Uncle Bill Hornickel

Back Porch Talkin'

I0143079

Livin' Country

William "Uncle Bill" Hornickel

BPT Publishing
Laconia, Indiana

ISBN: 0615604684
ISBN-13: 9780615604688

GIVIN' THANKS

First and foremost, I want to thank God for His grace and guidance. His divine presence makes all things possible, including Back Porch Talkin'.
Of course, I want to thank Carolyn, who is not just my wife and partner but my soul-mate. You, Me, We…We are…and forever shall be! You are my inspiration in life. I love you.
And all the rest: my family, friends, neighbors, and fans.
Your love, kindness, and support fuels me.

Uncle Bill Hornickel

DEDICATION

To Grandma Sylvetta Wright: at 100 years of age,
you inspire me to live. And to write.
This work is also dedicated to the loving memory of several very
special people in my life:
Grandma Alice Hornickel
Grandpa Carl Hornickel
Uncle Clarence Knear
Aunt Josephine Knear
Mother-in-law Martha Sprayberry Hitner Cabiness
Uncle Jim Correll
Uncle Kenneth Phillips
Lisa Ann Phillips
Alice Waters Kennedy

Table of Contents
Introduction

On the cover:
The top left photo is of a double rainbow over Grandma Hornickel's house where Back Porch Talkin' was born so long ago. Carolyn's mother, Martha, lived there from 2005 until her passing in the spring of 2011. This photo was taken on her birthday in the spring of 2010.

The top right photo of wild flowers growing along the country road was taken in the Kintner Bottoms near the historic Cedar Farms. Carolyn noticed their beauty and stopped for a picture.

The bottom photo was taken in 2007 of my dad, Ralph, and me heading out to pick up a load of straw with the old 50 John Deere. That's me behind the wheel.
All photos by Carolyn Hornickel (A/K/A- Aunt Carolyn)

A Special Thanks
A huge thanks to Carolyn Hornickel for her talents
in designing and laying out the cover. In addition, she is our webmaster, director of marketing, and head of promotions. She also serves as my editor-in-chief and head critic.
She is my creative consultant and my co-author.
She is my rock. Without her love, encouragement, and inspiration this book would have never become a reality. She is truly my partner in all that I do. She recognized my potential and pushed me to reach the stars!
You are amazing!
You...Me...We...We are!
And forever shall be!
I love you!

"Back Porch Talkin' isn't just a bunch of stories;
it is a way of life!"

Uncle Bill Hornickel

Back Porch Talkin'

Martha Sprayberry Hitner Cabiness was born in 1934 on a farm near the small town of Elizabeth, Indiana. She married at age 16 and eventually had four children, including her youngest, Carolyn Sue, who is now my wife. In 2010, I asked Martha to tell me what livin' country was like during her childhood. The following story is in her words.

Remembering the Ol' Seven Springs Place

Well, I tell ya it's like this...it was hard living down there; we didn't have much, but we made it just fine. We didn't have electricity or running water and the county came down to build us a nice outhouse...yes, an outhouse!

There was over 250 acres there with seven springs on it, that's where it got its name from, along with a tall, white, two-story farm house that had six rooms with one wood stove downstairs in the big room and a wood burning cook stove in the kitchen. The largest spring was about 500 feet from the house. You had to walk down a path across a creek, then through the woods, then over a spring branch walking on log, then up to the mouth of the large spring cave. That's where we kept our spring box which housed our milk and cream to keep it cold. My mom, Mary Langsdon Sprayberry, sold the cream to a truck that came by and picked it up.

The land belonged to Mr. and Mrs. Charlie Wren. I was between 10 and 11 years (1944-1945) when I lived on the seven springs place with my five younger siblings: Kenneth, Katherine, Helen, Orville, and Janie. My youngest sister, Dorothy "Janie" Sprayberry Howard, was born on the Seven Springs place. All of us were born at home; didn't go to a hospital back then to be brought into this world. That was some 62 years ago. My family owned 25 acres up the road at our old homestead at the top of the hill, but it just wasn't big enough to raise crops and a family on. My dad, Irvin Ira Sprayberry, was a hard working man; he raised all six of us kids, worked the farm and held a job all with just one arm. He lost his left arm crossing a barbed wire fence while hunting when he was 16 years old.

Dad rented the Seven Springs ground to raise tobacco, hay and corn. We lived in the ol' house for free. We lived there maybe, oh, 4 or 5 years before the Beagle Club took over to fence it all off to put rabbits in there to hold weekend rabbits hunts for hunters from Kentucky.

I can remember my brother, Kenneth, and I had goats that we would have to take out to the pastures to stake out with chains and one day my goat decided to take off running across the creek, but I held on, only to slip and fall into the creek cutting my right knee wide open and I still have the scar to this day. Mom said, "Well, if you weren't messing around, and paying more attention to what you were doing, you wouldn't have slipped and fell and cut your damned knee in the first place!" That was just how mom was.

We had cows, but the pasture wasn't fenced very good and these cows, one or two would get out and we would have to go way down the holler, where the big dam is now about a mile and a half away to the Kannapel farm just to get the cows. When we would bring them back dad would go get cow chains so we could stake them out in the pasture, staying with them all day long in the hot sun until their bellies got full and bring them back to the barn.

When it was time for me to go to school, which I really liked doing, I wasn't able to go as much as I wanted to because we had to work the farm. I really wanted to learn to play the piano but mom and dad couldn't afford to play for my piano lessons. We always had to miss school at the beginning of the school year to help with the tobacco, corn, and cutting wood for the winter. Dad would buy us all a new pair of shoes at the beginning of the school year and we wore those shoes until there was nothing left of them. I remember putting in a piece of cardboard just so my shoes would have a sole, then the sole would come loose and I would have to take some wire and wire them together.

Raising tobacco paid the taxes on the land and helped get us Christmas presents. I can remember in the winter time up at our old home place, we would have to put bone-dust sacks over our feet and up our legs tied with bailing string, to walk through the snow so we could cut trees down for fire wood and kindling. Dad was working night shift at Hoosier Panel in New Albany and renting a room above a tavern for a week then coming home on the weekends, so it was up to me and my brother to keep the house warm and take care of the farm and family while dad was gone. I learned which tree was which from my dad, being of Native American heritage and working in a saw mill.

One time, while Kenneth and I was cutting down trees with a cross cut saw, Kenneth wasn't pulling his end back, and boy, did that make me mad, so I decided I would get him good. I pushed down on my end of the long saw and the other end's handle smacked right up under his chin. He ran back to the house bawling. I didn't get no whipping though; I told mom the truth that he wasn't pulling his end of the saw. We had to cut wood almost every day because it was what mom cooked with and heated with.

My dad also worked on the county road and worked in the Steve Kirkham Saw Mill in Corydon and mom worked the farm feeding the chickens, cows, old hogs, and raising vegetables. Mom would go to Barnes' Store in Elizabeth to buy chicken feed in really pretty printed cloth sacks and my Aunt Bessy would wash the sacks, then make my sister, Katherine, dresses out of them so she'd have something nice to wear to school when she could go.

When the creek was up mom and dad couldn't cross it, they would have to walk all the way up to the Davis farm to get around it, then up to the barn to milk the cows, then they would carry the milk buckets back the same way they came.

We had a really nice barn with stables on both ends and two lofts. We had 3 or 4 cows on one side and at least two horses on the other side to plow the fields with.

It took two horses to pull the mowing machine that dad had to mow the hay. And then it took horses again to pull the hay rake with dad on it, to rake the hay in long rows, then my dad would hook the horses up to the hay wagon while we older kids walked beside the wagon with pitch forks to pitch the hay up on the wagon. Then we had to unload the hay into the loft by pitching it up there. I can remember the large, nice hay loft and us kids wallowing in the soft pile of hay then jumping off it to the floor below. It's a darn wonder we didn't break our legs.

In the fall, winter, and spring, we had to get up in the wee hours of the morning before we went to school to feed the cows, horses, hogs, and chickens, then milk the cows by hand into metal buckets. We had to carry the buckets across the creek up the narrow path to the house so mom could put the fresh milk into a cream separator; milk would come out one side and cream out the other, then we would carry the separated milk and cream in buckets back down across the creek and up the hill, through the woods across the creek log to the large mouth of the spring to put the milk and cream into the spring box to keep it cold. The largest spring had a large pool at the bottom of it and that is where we would get our water from, carrying heavy buckets back to the house.

Mom would plant pole beans in with the corn so the beans would climb up the corn stalks. We had a potato patch and the best blackberry patch down in the holler. Mom would can the beans, corn, and blackberries so we could have blackberry cobbler that mom would bake in a wood stove, which also heated our house in the winter. The potatoes were put into the smoke house under straw to keep them fresh all winter long.

When it came time to butchering a hog in the winter, we had to build a large fire to heat water in an old oil barrel, and then dad would get the gun, go kill the ol' hog, and cut its throat to make it bleed good. Then we all had to help get the old hog down in the barrel of hot boiling water to scald off the hair, pull it out, lay it on a wooden sled, scrape all the hair off with sharp knives. Then all of us helped dad lift the scalded, scraped hog up in the large oak tree with the single tree by its back feet. We'd put a wash tub under the hog and dad would cut the hog open to gut it and let it bleed out good. We all couldn't wait for mom to fix the liver for supper that night.

The hog would hang out there all day long, then in the evening we all helped take the hog into the smoke house for dad to cut it up into hams, shoulders, tenderloins, and side bacon while mom took the head, cooked it down and made head cheese. She would cook the ears, feet, and tail, then pickle them into jars and boy, was that good! The ribs and backbones we would use to make vegetable soup with. Mom would render up the rinds and fat of the hog to make cracklings or as most know as "pork rinds" and our cooking lard.

When mom didn't have any milk to make gravy or biscuits with, she would make what she called "some bitch bread" and gravy made with bacon grease, flour, and spring water, along with fried taters"

Now at 76 years old, remembering the old Seven Springs place has brought back into my mind a childhood I'll never forget and sometime I would like to go back there and maybe, just maybe I'll start taking piano lessons now.

Eight months after Mother shared this story for our book, she was called home to be with God. We will never forget her love and kindness, or the humble woman she was. We miss her dearly. In our hearts, we know that she is indeed, back there at the Old Seven Springs place once again. The last five years of her life, she lived in my Grandma Hornickel's house just across the county road from ours. It is so appropriate that her last years were spent there as it was Grandma's place that provided the inspiration for Back Porch Talkin'. Martha's recollection of her childhood on the Seven Springs place was told in the same way that folks used to while sitting on the back porch with friends and neighbors.

That's what Back Porch Talkin' is: gathering on the back porch with your friends and neighbors, sharing stories, telling a few tall-tales, and maybe even sharing a recipe or two. And it was a place to reminisce about days gone by and those folks from our past who are no longer with us. That is why I decided to begin this book with mother's story of her childhood. She, like so many others in my life, understood the importance of keeping those old memories alive and passing them on for future generations to learn from. Thank you, Martha Louise Sprayberry Hitner Cabiness for sharing your livin' country memories with us. I am dedicating this book to Martha's memory. She believed in Back Porch Talkin'. Hopefully, you will, too.

Back Porch Talkin'

Howdy! Welcome to Back Porch Talkin'! I'm Uncle Bill and I am mighty glad you stopped by! Come on in, pull up a chair and sit a spell. Has it really been that long ago when folks would visit with their neighbors? Out here in the country, taking time out to visit with neighbors, well, that was just a way of life and it's a life that I sure do miss!

I grew up in the country and I still live in the country, about half way between the small, rural towns of Elizabeth and Laconia in southern Indiana. In fact, I only live about a quarter of a mile from the farm where I was born and raised. Well, I wasn't actually born there; I was born in a hospital in Corydon, Indiana, but it sounds so much more nostalgic to say, "I was born and raised there." Unlike so many of my childhood friends who couldn't wait to grow up so they could get out of the country, I couldn't wait to grow up so I could *stay* in the country. I love it here; always have and always will.

Back in the days before email, cell phones, and texting, about the only way to share news and gossip in the country was an honest-to-goodness, old-fashioned, face-to-face, in-the-flesh conversation. Around here, folks would often "go visitin'" which was just a polite way of saying, "lets go over to so-an-so's house and catch up on the latest gossip." Many is the evening that I can recollect being at my Grandma Hornickel's when someone would stop by to just sit for a spell and "visit." We'd all sit around on the porch and the older folks would talk about the weather, the crops, politics, and whatever else happened to come up. Most of the time, however, they'd end up talking about other folks that they knew or recalling things that happened way back when. And that is how I learned all about our local history and my rural heritage: by listening to the older folks sitting on the back porch talkin'.

For example, when I was around eight years old, I learned that my grandpa's brother used to haul his grain into New Albany to the elevator with a four-horse team pulling two box wagons. Then, after he got his money for the grain, he'd stop off at a tavern and spend half of his money lying around with the old harlots who hung out in there. I found this to be very fascinating *and* educational, despite the fact that I didn't have a clue what a harlot was or why he'd want to lay around with them. In fact, I doubt that I even knew what a tavern was but the fact still remains that I did learn *something* about my rural heritage and history.

Not all of the talkin' done on the back porch was gossip. Uncle Charlie Knear stopped in at Grandma's one evening and he told a story about the time that George Flannigan was fishing for catfish down in the Ohio River and caught one that weighed over sixty pounds! Uncle Charlie said it was so big, old George had to use his old John Deere tractor just to pull it up onto the bank. I sat there, eyes wide open and speechless (*a rarity for me*), when Grandma asked what they did with a fish that big. Uncle Charlie leaned back and said, "Well, old George Flannigan ended up throwing it back 'cause everybody knows them river cats ain't fit to eat!" My immediate question was why Old George Flannigan was fishing in the Ohio River for catfish in the first place if river cats ain't fit to eat? Never did get an answer to that question. Uncle Charlie swore that it was all true, but even at that age, I could recognize a good tall-tale when I heard one. And that's just another example of what folks talked about on the back porch.

Of course, sometimes my grandma would be the one who would go visitin'. In the summer, I might spend the better part of the week at grandma's house helping her mow grass, tend the garden, or trudge off into the cow pasture to pick blackberries. With my grandma, each day was always an adventure, that much was for certain. After supper, she'd come into the living room and tell me to get washed up and put on some clean clothes because we were going to take a ride which was Grandma's secret code word for "going visitin." We'd head off on some unfamiliar country road until she'd pull into someone's drive. Then we'd get out of the car and usually end up sitting on someone else's back porch, talkin'. If it was a good night, we might end up visiting at two different places before retuning home. I always liked it when we'd stop in at her Cousin Ed's place because his wife, Lillian, would always give me a bowl of ice cream or some cookies to eat while I listened to their conversations, which was the best part of the whole experience.

And that's just what the back porch was for: sharing some news and gossip, telling a few tall-tales and funny stories, trading recipes and gardening secrets, or just reminiscing about the good old days. For nearly a half of a century, I have experienced back porch talkin'; first as a passive listener and then later as an active participant. What follows in this book is my interpretation of what growing up and living country is all about. Some of the stories are true accounts of actual events and some are based on tall-tales that I have heard throughout my life. In addition, I have included some good old-fashioned, down-home recipes of country dishes that I grew up enjoying, some homespun philosophy for you to ponder, and you'll even get to meet a couple of real-rural characters; two very close friends of mine, Wally and Maynard. And no country experience would be complete without a few stories about the signature icon of agriculture, the farm tractor.

So sit back and relax. Things always move a little slower in the country and thanks for stopping by to visit with us on The Back Porch Talkin'!

Livin' Country

Back Porch Talkin'

Rocket Ride

I grew up in the country on a large farm, which by definition makes me a "farm-boy." It was a life that was filled many adventures and experiences. Some of my first responsibilities on the farm included taking care of livestock and by the time I was in the second grade, I was responsible for feeding and watering the sows in the farrowing building each day when I arrived home from school. My summers were filled with caring for baby pigs, checking on the market hogs, and hoeing in the tobacco patch. When I reached the age of ten, my dad decided I was ready to learn the art of solo tractor driving. I started out with the simple operations first: piloting the tractor at the break-neck speed of 2 miles per hour through the hay fields while the hired hands, high school boys mostly, pitched the bales up on the wagon for my dad to stack. By the time I was thirteen, I was plowing with a 10-ton green and yellow John Deere into the long, cool Indiana nights. Looking back, it was a tremendous responsibility for a young teen, though at the time I didn't understand that. It was just "life on the farm."

Hogs and large farm machinery filled my world and I loved it! There was, however, one area of farm life that I didn't have much exposure to and that was the world of horses. Oh sure, we had a horse on our farm. He was a twenty year-old retired barrel racer, a Pinto Paint Quarter horse named Rocket. The horse had earned the right to live out his life on our farm, grazing in the pastures with the cattle. When I was about four, I remember my dad putting the saddle on Rocket and taking me for my first ride in the snow and I loved the view from up there. Old Rocket was a good natured, gentle animal that loved people almost as much as he did wandering through the pastures grazing on grass. He had only one bad characteristic; he really wasn't what you would call a "pleasure rider." My dad said he was a "speed horse" though I never really understood what that meant.

I was enlightened the hard way one summer when I was about twelve. It was one of those boring, lazy, summer days. I had finished all of the chores my dad had left for me and I was looking

13

for some excitement. Rocket had wandered into the barn to beat the summer heat and I was sitting on a bale of hay talking to him when it suddenly occurred to me that I should saddle the old horse up and go for a ride. Mind you, I had never been on Rocket alone in my young life. My reasoning told me that if I was old enough to drive a tractor and operate heavy farm machinery, then surely I was old enough to operate a horse. Besides, I had watched plenty of episodes of *Bonanza* and *Gunsmoke* on TV, so I knew all I needed to know about riding a horse.

I walked Rocket out into the driveway of the barn and heaved the old brown saddle up onto his back. I did my best to mimic my dad's actions of cinching the saddle down and then put the bridle and bit on the horse's head. I stood back and surveyed my saddling job. Satisfied, I put my foot into the stirrup and climbed up on Rocket's back. I could feel my heart pounding in my chest as I turned Rocket and walked him out into the barnyard and then into the grass of our front yard. We just slowly walked around for about twenty minutes. My mother came running out of the house in hysterics yelling to "get off of that horse before you get killed!" Golly, Mom...it is just a horse! See? I am a natural! A regular Hoss Cartwright.

I walked him back into the barn and climbed down. My first check-out ride was complete and in my mind, I was now a bona fide cowboy. I put Rocket back into the pasture and went back to my usual summer-time activities of shooting some barn-yard hoops and messing around in the in the hog house. Pigs, I had learned, made great playmates when there was no one else around. At very least, they listened intently to my stories and I really appreciated that. Later that evening, when dad arrived home from his day job at the University of Louisville, I told him all about my big horsey adventure. I was not met with a proud smile of fatherly approval but a frown and a harsh warning:
"You'd better stay off of that damned horse. You don't know the first damn thing about riding. He isn't your normal horse! Your mother broke her leg when you were a baby trying to ride Rocket. You're gonna get your ass hurt!"

I could see dad was not going to be supportive of my new

status as an old cow poke, so I dropped the subject.

The next day, I decided to throw caution to the wind and show them just how wrong they were. I decided go for a real ride. Again, I saddled Rocket and climbed up onto his back. This time, however, my heart wasn't racing like the day before. Why should it? I was a pro now...just like the Lone Ranger. My mind was filled with great visions of riding Rocket to all ends of our expansive farm, exploring and finding new adventures, maybe even an over-night camping trip, just like in the movies.

I again turned Rocket out into the barnyard and this time I reached my booted feet back and gouged Rocket in the flanks. Roughly three seconds later, I decided I needed to rethink this cowboy thing.

If it is possible for a twenty-some year-old horse to go from zero to sixty, then Rocket must have been up for the task because all I can remember is watching objects in the yard pass by in a blur as we headed out into the hay field in front of our house. There was one thing I did learn rather quickly and that is there is a huge difference in the way it feels on your backside from when a horse walks slowly around in the yard and when he is running at top speed across a hay field. I suppose there was one positive to all of this; I must have done a reasonably good job of cinching the saddle because it was staying put which was a good thing since it was all that was prohibiting me from finding out what it truly felt like to fly.

The end of the hay field was rapidly approaching and I was curiously beginning to wonder where we were going to go next. I was already convinced that Rocket had decided to run the 200 miles to Lexington, Kentucky where he was from because he made no indication of slowing down. Along about this time, I returned enough of my brain capacity from the level of terror I was currently in to that of semi-rational thought. It suddenly occurred to me that gripped in my white-with-fear hands were the reins and that all I needed to do was turn Rocket back toward the house.

It is truly amazing how much one can learn from a new experience. Again, I was educated on just how a barrel racer responds to the slight pulling of the reins to one side or another.

As the end of the field neared, I tugged the leather straps in my trembling hand sharply to the left.

The previous summer I had felt the exhilaration of riding the Tilt-a-Whirl at the county fair and was glad that they had a bar across your lap to hold you in the seat as the car spun around on a dime. At that moment, I was wishing that horses came with a similar bar because I saw the blurring world spin one hundred and eighty degrees around me and distinctly remember holding on to the saddle horn as if it were welded to my hands. Apparently, old retired horses don't know that they are retired or even old for that matter because Rocket found a bit more speed after he executed that stand-on-a-dime turn. Within seconds, the hay field disappeared and the yard was back under us. I quickly began to wonder where we were headed next because there was a fence on the far side of the yard and I remember thinking that it would be a real hoot if Rocket decided to become a jumper in his old age. The time had definitely come for me to end my career as a cowboy.

Maybe it was dumb luck or maybe it was the Good Lord looking out for a really dumb country kid but from somewhere in the depths of my adolescent brain came the realization that horses are supposed to stop when you holler "WHOA!"

I pulled back on the reins and screamed out the command. Just as suddenly as he had taken off, Rocket applied full brakes. The ride was over. Please exit to the left. Please remember to collect your stomach, lunch, and guts as you depart. Thank you for flying Rocket Airlines.

I slid down off of Rocket and just kind of collapsed in the yard. Rocket began casually eating grass as if nothing had just transpired and I rolled over onto my back and stared up at the clouds slowly drifting along. I really wanted to get up but my rubbery legs were still numb with fear so I just laid there trying to decide if I was still in one piece. From the time I had gouged Rocket in the flanks until that moment, less than 60 seconds had passed. It was then and there that I decided that my one-minute of horsemanship would probably be enough to pacify me for the rest of my life.

Slowly, I got up and walked over to Rocket, grabbed the reins and led him back to the barn. I eventually did get the nerve to get back up on Rocket again, but I learned a couple valuable lessons from that first experience.

First, never assume that you know what you're doing from just watching TV; and second, don't EVER gouge a speed horse in the flanks with your boot heels unless you're ready to take a real Rocket ride!

The Cry of the Auctioneer

When it comes to rural characters, some of the most memorable are the men who stand up on a platform and chant out requests for bids on items for sale. Sorry, I have yet to meet a legitimate female auctioneer; it appears to be a male dominated business.

From the earliest days of American history, auctioneers have played a key role in rural heritage and commerce. From the dark days of slave auctions to the modern world of estate liquidation; there is something artistic, poetic, and yes, mesmerizing about the chant and cry of an auctioneer at work. And for most of us who grew up in the country, auctioneers are icons; symbols of rural commerce and traditionalism that possess the unique ability to mix property, rapid-fire language, wit, and personality into a unique, exciting buying experience.

I remember the first auction that I ever attended. I was only about five or six and it was an estate auction of a local old farmer who had passed away. The Ladies Aid of the Rehoboth Presbyterian Church was providing the food and drinks for the event, which meant my Grandma Hornickel was there helping sell hot dogs, chili, sloppy joes, and pie to the attendees. I found a perch near the machinery row to watch and listen in absolute amazement as Auctioneer Sam Wolfe chanted and cried out dollar figures and quick one-liners in a rapid-fire monotone song while men in overalls and seed corn caps stood stoically in a cluster, occasionally nodding or slightly raising one finger in the air.

"Okay. Up next we have a 1948 Farmall. Hey! Lookie here! You're not gonna find a tractor in this good of shape anywhere else but right here! This one's ready to go home with you today and go right to work! This ones so pretty, you could probably even get your wife to drive it," old Sam cackled. And then he began his chant. "Who is gonna get us started here? Hey alright! I have 250! Now who is gonna give me 275?"

His voice was thin and nasally as he chanted out words and numbers in a bizarre song that occasionally contained recognizable speech. As the song continued and the numbers

18

climbed, fewer and fewer hands raised until Sam narrowed the bidding down to two individuals. Then he really went to work, taunting each to not be out bid by the other until finally, the bids ceased. Then he made a couple of final pleas.

"I need 875...anyone gonna give 875? I need 875...875...875?"

In the momentary silence no one breathed as time hung in the balance of the pending sale. Sam finally yelled out "SOLD!" and the men shuffled and shifted and murmured among themselves as he moved to the next piece of machinery that was up for sale. Then, as Sam began crying again, all movement again stopped and the group of men once again became still and motionless, as if the slightest body movement would be mistaken for a bid.

Over the next few years, I was fortunate enough to experience this phenomenon many more times. Even as a young boy, I found it interesting how different auctioneers would mix humor and conversation into their chant of numbers. Of course, at that age, I didn't recognize that sometimes these auctions were emotional events for family members who were watching a lifetime of property and treasure being sold off, piece-by-piece, to the highest bidder. I probably didn't comprehend that this was a fiscal transaction taking place; I was only interested in listening to the voice of the auctioneer as he cried out his long chant of numbers that eventually concluded with an exclamation of "SOLD!" before pausing and then beginning again.

And then, when I was ten, I got to experience the auction phenomenon from a new perspective: that of the seller. It was my first year in 4-H and I showed a market hog at the county fair. On Friday night of the fair, after all of the judging had taken place, 4-H livestock exhibitors would sell their show animals in the annual 4-H livestock auction. Local auctioneers volunteered their services to help the us sell our animals and earn some extra cash for our future endeavors. I was shaking with fear as the arena door slid back and I drove my barrow hog into the small, fenced area in front of the announcer's stand.

Meredith Meyers of New Middletown was the auctioneer on the stand when I came out with my hog. I heard him say my name over the loudspeaker and he said, "Now, here is a young man who

needs to make some money tonight! Let's help him out." And he
began chanting out numbers that I couldn't quite make out as I
drove my hog from one end of the small arena to the other. As he
began to slow down in his song, suddenly he leaned down over
the announcers stand and said to me, "Give 'em all a big smile and
let 'em know you're not ready to quit!" I turned and did my best to
smile at the big crowd of business men and interested on-lookers
in the 4-H show barn. Without warning, his chanting began once
again, and he got even louder. The whole event lasted only a
minute or two but for me, it seemed like forever. Finally, he
shouted out the signature "Sold for one-twenty-nine per pound!"

Both me and my hog (well, someone's hog) were herded out
the other side of the sale arena. My dad was there as I drove my
hog back to the pen and he said, "Well, you're 367 dollars richer!" I
couldn't believe my ears! The most money I had ever had in my
possession was fifty bucks. And now, just like that, I had 367
dollars! My dad told me to make sure that I thanked the buyer,
Gehlbach & Royse Funeral Home. Gee! That was creepy; the
funeral home bought my pig! I made my way out into the sea of
buyers and thanked Roger Royse, the stoic, stone-faced owner.
But my real hero was auctioneer Meredith Meyers. He didn't give
up when the bidding got slow; instead, he used his charm and
quick-wit to help get the bidding started again and made me a few
more dollars for my bank account.

Of course, my most exciting auction moment came a couple of
years later when I was twelve. I wanted to show a calf at the fair
that year, a first for me. My dad took me to a 4-H cattle sale in the
fall. He said that I could take some of the money that I had in the
bank from selling my 4-H hogs the previous two years and use it to
purchase a yearling heifer to show the following summer. We
arrived at the sale barn, signed in to receive a buyer's number and
then went to the barn area where we perused all of the prospects.
Once we had selected a few heifers that we wanted to bid on, we
took our seats in the auction barn. The sale started and the
auctioneer began chanting and the barkers (the guys who stand
around the edge of the sale arena and look for bids) were shouting
"YEAH!" I was again mesmerized by the experience. Then, the first

heifer on our list was run into the arena. My dad causally handed the buyers flag (the card with our bidder's number on it) to me and said, "It's your money and your cow...you do the bidding." My blood turned to ice; my feet and hands went numb. I was shaking with fear! I just sat there, frozen! The auctioneer was chanting and the barkers were yelling. Bids were coming from everywhere in the barn. Everywhere except from me, that is. My dad leaned to me and said, "Bid! Bid! You're gonna lose it!" I couldn't get my arm to move; I was absolutely paralyzed with fear. All of the sudden, my dad grabbed my arm and lifted it high above my head. The barker on our side of the barn saw my arm and screamed out, "YEAH!" And suddenly, I was in the game!

Roughly one minute and ten bids later, I was 335 dollars poorer and 1 heifer richer! "WOW," I exclaimed, "That was fun!" My dad then explained to me that there is an art to buying at an auction. He said it was all about timing and playing the other bidders. So I began watching very closely and studying the whole process.

About a half of an hour later, my dad leaned over to me and said, "Well, what the hell? Let's buy a feeder steer, too! I'll pay for it; you bid on it." And I did, too! A brown and white Simmental steer to go with the heifer I had just bought.

As we pulled out of the sale area that night in the truck with my newly purchased animals safely tucked away in the trailer, I felt as if I had made the passage from childhood to adulthood. I had actually purchased something at an auction! Not once, but twice! And in a peculiar way, I felt like more of a man. The auctioneer had taken my bid; I had played the ultimate adult buying game; I was a bidder!

Since that time, I have attended many auctions: livestock auctions, property auctions, charity auctions, tractor auctions, and even an art auction. Sometimes I have been a bidder; sometimes not. I have even got to serve as a barker on a couple of occasions (boy, was that fun!). Today's auctioneers utilize the latest in technology: laptop computers, wireless microphones, online bidding, and a whole bunch of other neat gadgets. But one thing remains the same: when the auctioneer begins chanting, the war between bidders is on until one person is declared the winner. And to the victor go the spoils, after he or she has paid for their purchase, of course. Now days, the local auctioneering firm extraordinaire around these parts is the father-and-son team of Paul and Brian Beckort of Laconia, Indiana. They have taken the auctioneering business into the 21st century with on-line inventory and bid registration, on-sight credit card acceptance, and a mobile office facility. However, with all of that modern technology, one thing remains constant: When the chanting begins, all eyes and ears are on the man standing up on the platform with the microphone. He is the authority of the sale; the arbitrator between bidders; the referee of instant commerce. He is the auctioneer!

If you have never been to a rural auction, you owe it to yourself to attend just for the experience of the atmosphere and the excitement. You don't have to buy a thing. Just stand around and watch and listen. But don't be surprised if you don't come home with a treasure or two. That is the mark of a good auctioneer; he'll make you feel good about buying something you didn't even know you wanted. And besides, part of the fun of owning the treasure is winning it fair and square. The auctioneer said so!

Don't Hatch Your Chickens Before You Count

I guess those of us who were raised in the country take for granted just how challenging this way of life can really be. After all, we were born with the smell of manure in our noses and the itch of hay in our pants. Most of us farm folks learned to drive a tractor well before we learned to drive a car and we were using machinery that could mangle the human body in seconds before most city kids were even allowed to get within ten feet of a lawn mower. This is our world and we have spent a lifetime learning it; it is a part of who and what we are. I am not in any way putting the urbanites down; they can't help it that they were raised in a different environment. But let's face it; there is nothing more entertaining for us country folks than to watch the city folks attempt to make the transition from city to country.

For all of you who are reading this who were born in the city and then made the move to the country I want to assure you: I am about to poke fun at you. I am in no way making an apology here. After all, we didn't ask you to move out here and invade the country so we reserve the right to laugh our butts off at your expense. If any of us ever move from the country to the city, then you can snicker at our ignorance all day long. Write and publish a book that celebrates the nostalgic history and heritage of city life and make fun of us backwoods hillbilly folks until the cows come home...ooops...until the garbage truck rumbles past. Whatever.

The first real revelation that city folks have when they move out to the country to live that simple, country life is that country life is anything but simple. Even with all of the modern conveniences, country living takes a little getting used to, especially if you're going to try your hand at "becoming a real farmer." A prime example of this is the couple that moved out here to the country from New York City. Both were raised in Lower Manhattan and were from rather well-to-do families, which you'd have to be if you lived in Lower Manhattan. They were in their early thirties and had decided that before they started a family, they wanted to get away from the big city and move to the country.

The husband, Jim, had attended Harvard and his roommate

was a fellow from rural Indiana, who had oddly enough decided that he wanted to get out of the sticks and move to the big city. Hey, it happens. During their years at Harvard, the country fellow had turned his city boy roommate on to the music of John Mellencamp, who, as you may know, grew up in a rural area just outside of Seymour, Indiana. Now, everybody knows that listening to John Mellencamp's music will magically transform you from a city-slicker into a country hayseed overnight, especially if you listen to *Small Town* over and over until you really believe that you were really born in a small town.

Anyway, after listening to the country boy's music and hearing him talk about what it was like to grow up in the country, this New York City boy decided that someday he wanted to move to Indiana and live out in the sticks. By the time he was thirty-three, he had made enough money on Wall Street to afford to purchase a small farm, and naturally it had to be in rural Indiana. And so, he and his city bride of five years packed up their belongings and moved to their newly purchased 25-acre farm located between Lanesville and Elizabeth. And here is where the fun really began.

After settling in to their new home, a 75 year-old, two-story, remodeled farmhouse, they set out to become real country people. They did what they thought every good rural dwellers should do; they subscribed to *The Mother Earth News* and *Small Farm* magazines to learn all that they needed to know about raising a garden, keeping chickens, and raising livestock. Here is where having a good deal of money at your disposal can get you into trouble. Now, most true country folks know if you're going raise chickens to produce eggs for your own use, then you're probably better off just buying a few layers from a mail order hatchery. This couple, however, purchased a 96-egg incubator out of one of their magazines and then ordered *8 dozen* fertile eggs. You know those Wall Street folks; they do everything to excess. Following the instructions that came with the incubator, they proceeded to load all 96 eggs in there and turn it on.

21 days later, much to their joy and amazement, the eggs began to hatch. At first, the wife, Lisa, was just like a new mother, taking the little chicks as they hatched and moving them into a box. To

keep the new chicks warm, she pulled out a new electric blanket and put it in the bottom of the box. But then the box began to fill up and she had to spread out the king-size electric blanket on the kitchen floor and use suitcases and anything else she could find to make a chick corral. Out of 96 eggs in the incubator, 88 hatched. Apparently, they had not received the issue of *The Mother Earth News* that discussed putting baby chicks under a brooder light until they are old enough to be on their own, nor did they have any idea of what baby chicks eat. Not knowing what else to do, Jim had to break down and go to the local feed and farm store to find out what to do with all of those baby chicks.

This is where I enter into the story, cause I was the guy who owned the feed and farm store. Jim came walking in wearing a pair of Italian dress shoes that had a crust of mud around the soles, wool suit pants, and pale blue dress shirt with a silk tie. He looked like he should have been on the cover of *GQ* except for the fact he had chick droppings all over his pale blue shirt. He nervously walked up to the counter and started telling me his baby chick problem, describing in detail how they had 88 hungry baby chicks running around on the electric blanket-covered kitchen floor.

Eugene Gleitz was in the store telling stories that day, as usual. Now, Eugene is a real country character. He always has a solution for any problem that someone may have; however, you are always forced to listen to at least three of his stories just to get to the resolution and even then you might not be too sure of just how the stories pertain to your immediate situation. He was dressed in his usual daily attire of faded, well-worn overalls with an old Pioneer seed corn cap perched on his head. His long, emotionless face was highlighted by the dark frame glasses hanging from his nose. When Jim began explaining his situation, I glanced at Eugene and sure enough, his ears had perked up like a dog on the hunt as he tuned in on the conversation.

After he had described his dilemma, Jim looked at me and then at Eugene with a face full of hopeless desperation. Before I could respond, Eugene began in his usual slow drawl that dripped of country twang like a homemade biscuit covered with black molasses.

"How many of them eggs did you say hatched," Eugene asked. When Jim replied "88," Eugene got that little grin on his face that he would get when he knew he was about to have fun with someone.

"How many eggs are you'all planning to eat every day?"

Jim shrugged and said, "I don't know…how many will the chickens lay?" So we tried to explain to Jim that once chickens get old enough to start laying, they could expect 1 to 2 eggs a day from each hen.

Jim's eyes got as big as saucers and he asked, "You mean we could be getting 100 eggs a day? What are we gonna do with a 100 eggs a day?"

Eugene's eyes twinkled as he drawled, "Wellll, don't worry about thaat…at least half of those chicks are probably roosters anyway. By the time you separate them out to raise and kill, you'll probably only have about 40 layers. Once they get settled into layin', they'll only produce one a day. That's just 280 eggs a week. That ain't that many."

City Boy Jim's eyes got even wider as he stared at Eugene. "What in the hell are we supposed to do with all of those dead roosters after we kill them? And just how do you kill them, anyway? I don't own a gun or anything."

Eugene looked at me and I could tell he was about to laugh out loud and so I said, "Well, you generally just take a hatchet and chop their heads off. Then, you'll need to scald them in hot water so their feathers will pull out easily. After that, you just gut them, wash them real good, and put them down in ice water for a few hours. That will give you enough time to clean the livers and the gizzards. Then you can wrap them and put them in the freezer."

I looked at Jim. His face had turned a pale, greenish color and his hands were shaking. He looked at me and then at Eugene and then in the most serious tone I have ever heard, he asked, "What do we do with all of the dead roosters once we have them in the freezer?" That was it. Eugene and I could not hold back any longer. We laughed so hard that Jim started getting mad. When I was finally able to get my breath again and stop the convulsing in my gut, I apologized for laughing. Jim just frowned and then asked again, "What do we do with all of those dead roosters in the freezer?"

I cleared my throat and said, "Well, you eat them."

Jim had the most confused expression on his face as he looked back at me and asked, "You mean you can eat dead chickens?"

Eugene looked at me, his face all glowing and red as his whole body shook with laughter. He looked at Jim and cackled, "Haven't you ever eaten at Kentucky Fried Chicken? They don't fry those chickens alive!"

Now red-faced with embarrassment, Jim looked across that counter at me and quietly said, "I didn't know that egg chickens and eating chickens were the same thing. Honestly."

And that is when I knew that John Mellencamp was a piss-poor song writer. In all of those songs about small towns and scarecrows and stuff, he really should have had a song to tell all of the city folks that egg chickens and eating chickens are one in the same!

Poor old Jim, he just stood there at the counter looking so pathetic, still covered in embarrassment and chick droppings as Eugene launched into a story about the time Ed Mengus hatched a duckling that only had one leg. It seems as if this duck learned to hop around on that one leg like a kid on a pogo stick. I just shook my head and sat back down in my chair behind the counter, knowing that we'd have to listen to all of this story and two more before I could attempt to help Jim with his problem. Oh well, anyone dumb enough to get themselves into this kind of predicament should have to listen to three of Eugene Gleitz's stories!

Jim and Lisa finally found a local farmer who was willing to take all of the chicks and put them in the large brooder that he had in his chicken house. When the chicks got old enough to sex, he gave a dozen females back to the city folks to finish raising for layers. A few months after those chickens started laying, Jim stopped in the store one day to buy a couple bags of chicken feed. As I was loading the feed into the trunk of his BMW, he asked me if I sold a lot of chicken feed. "Oh, probably a couple tons or so every month," I answered. "Why do you ask?"

He shook his head and said, "Well, I just can't understand why anyone would raise their own eggs. It is costing us at least 30 dollars a month to feed these stupid chickens and we probably don't use more than four dozen eggs a month. I tried selling the extras but I can only get a dollar a dozen. I am going in the hole on this deal! How in the world can anyone make a living farming?"

And that just goes to show you that if a Wall Street banker can't make money farming, then perhaps Wall Street should just let the real experts, the farmers, handle the business of farming. Besides, real farmers just listen to John Mellencamp for entertainment; not advice on farming. And we don't read *The Mother Earth News,* either!

The Magic of Reverend Wayne Haun

Over the years, we have had many new neighbors move out here to the country. Some have made the transition to rural life just fine and others, well, they stayed for a while and then just moved on. I guess that is one reason that those of us who have lived here our whole lives tend to be a bit stand-offish toward the newcomers at first. It is kind of like making a pet out of a pig you intend to make into ham and sausage; when the day comes to have him butchered, you find that you're too attached to the animal. Oh, you still have him butchered, but every time you have ham for dinner, you're reminded of that cute little pig face.

New neighbors to the country are a bit like that; they move in and you make friends with them and then one day they pull up stakes and move on. It is just easier to keep your distance and avoid feelings of loss when they do move on. Of course, every once in a while you'll get a new neighbor that is just so darn friendly and likable that you just can't help but develop a friendship with them.

Once when I was a teenager, we got some new neighbors who were like that. I came down the road one day on a tractor and noticed that a new mobile home was being put in on the little lot just up the road from our farm. My Grandma Hornickel, who had no problem getting on the phone and calling anyone and everyone to find out information, soon discovered who our new neighbors were: Wayne and Donna Haun. Wayne, who had just graduated from the seminary, was the new minister at the Elizabeth First Baptist Church. His wife, Donna, was a secretary and had managed to get transferred to a company in downtown Louisville near the advertising agency where my mother worked. They were a young couple, not yet thirty and this was Wayne's first, permanent preaching assignment.

When I first heard that Wayne was a First Baptist minister, I figured that he was probably just another radical, fire-and-brimstone, pulpit-pounder so I made up my mind to just steer clear of him. One day right after they moved in, I drove past their trailer and noticed Wayne out in the yard washing his car and I was a bit shocked. He was wearing an old tie-dyed tee-shirt and cut-off blue jeans. He had a ball cap pulled down on his head with long, brown hair hanging out from underneath. But most shocking of all was the car he was washing: a cranberry red, 1970 Chevy Chevelle Super Sport with a big black racing stripe running up over the hood, top and trunk lid. It was out-fitted with Craigar rims, Goodyear Racing Eagles, and chrome thrush pipes. As I rode past gawking, he turned and flashed a big, warm smile and waved heartily. "Holy Cow (pardon the pun)," I thought. "This guy doesn't look like a typical preacher!"

Most of the preachers that I had been exposed to were much older men who always looked like they were ready to whip your ass at a moment's notice, especially if you were some smart-mouthed, long-haired teenager. I know it was probably my perception, but most old-school, country preachers were usually very stoic and reverent, almost to an obsession. Of course, I used to think that the phrase "Bible Belt" meant getting slapped upside the head with the Good Book, just to keep your ass in line. At any rate, this "Wayne Haun" fellow didn't fit the physical mold of a typical country church preacher, especially one of the First Baptist persuasion.

A few days later, we were baling hay at my grandma's place and I had to take a wagon load down to our farm to unload in the barn. Several of the hired hands climbed up on the loaded wagon and we started down the road. As we rode past our new neighbor's trailer, I noticed he was out in his front yard digging an old flowerbed. Smiling, he looked up and waved. Then he yelled out, "Looks like you're working hard today!"

I laughed smugly and then yelled back, "Hell yeah! We could use some help if you ain't afraid to get dirty!" All of the guys on the wagon laughed and I felt pretty good 'cause I said "hell" and made fun of the long-haired preacher. He laughed as we rode on by his yard, which made me a bit uneasy. I made fun of him and he is laughing?

After I had pulled the wagon loaded with hay into the barn, I climbed down from the tractor and walked around to the back as the hired hands began climbing up into the loft. Just then, I heard a car pull into the drive of the farm. I turned to see that candy apple red Chevelle pull up to the barn and Preacher Wayne climb out with a pair of brown jersey gloves on his hands.

"You want me to throw off or stack," he asked as he started up the wagon load of hay. Before I could answer, he began pitching bales from the top of the wagon over into the loft while the hired hands began stacking. "What is this guy up to," I wondered. "Shit! I'll bet he is going to start preaching to us young hooligans right there in the damned barn!" I shook my head and climbed up on the wagon with him and together we unloaded over a hundred bales of hay.

In the course of the afternoon I learned that he had spent six years in the air force before attending the seminary in Tennessee. He said he had learned to pitch hay when he was a boy to make money and he always enjoyed working on farms. He went on to say he felt lucky to be assigned to a church in a rural area because he really enjoyed living in the country. Well, Amen to that!

At the end of the day, just as we were unloading the last of the hay, he turned to me and said he wanted to ask me a question. I thought, "Oh boy! Here it comes! We're going get a sermon in the barn!"

He said, "I was wondering if I could get a few bales of hay from you in exchange for helping this afternoon?"

I looked at him puzzled and said, "Sure. What do you need hay for?"

He hesitated and then said, "For my big, white rabbit that I use in my magic act."

I know the look on my face must have been priceless. "Magic act," I asked skeptically.

He explained that in the seminary they encouraged students to learn an alternate trade to supplement their income because preaching wasn't always a high-paying profession, especially in a smaller congregation, so he had taken up magic. He then reached into the pocket of his blue jeans and pulled out a quarter. "Hold out your hand," he said. I obliged as I wondered what he was up to. He said, "Now, look here. I have a single quarter." He tossed it back and forth from one hand to another to emphasize that fact.

He then flipped the coin high up into the air, caught it, and then slapped it down on my hand, covering it with his. He said, "Now, close your hand up and hold that quarter real tight." By this time, all of the other guys who had been helping with the hay had gathered around to watch. "The thing about money is you never seem to have enough," he said. He reached out and tapped my fist with his finger and then asked, "So what are you going to do with that extra dollar and a quarter you just made?" I opened my clenched fist and low and behold, there was a neatly folded dollar bill resting on top of the quarter. How in the hell did he do that? And that was my introduction to the Reverend Wayne Haun. Oh, by the way...he never did do any preaching or praying the whole time we worked putting up hay.

Over the course of the next few months, I would occasionally stop by to see Wayne and we became pretty good friends. His wife and my mom started car-pooling to work each day and they began attending some of our family get-togethers. The interesting part of all of this is we aren't Baptists nor did we attend his church. And he never once tried to get us to attend even though my mom did start going occasionally to support is wife, Donna. It seems as if the old bitty-bags at the First Baptist Church were being a bit cold-shouldered towards her so my mom would go on Sundays and sit with her while Wayne preached.

A few months later, on a cold and snowy January day, Wayne came driving into our farm in his Chevelle. I was grinding a batch of hog feed in our big grinder-mixer as he came over and asked if I knew anything about the two old guys who were always walking up and down the county road. I thought for a moment and then replied, "Oh, you must mean the Maddox brothers, Kenny and Lloyd. Why do you ask?" He then told me one of the best country preacher stories I believe I have ever heard.

Wayne had gone to the church that morning to work on his sermon for Sunday. After he finished, he got in his Chevelle and headed back home. Just as he turned onto the county road from the state highway, he saw old Kenny and Lloyd walking along in the freezing cold carrying two bags of groceries each. Neither was dressed very warmly and he felt so sorry for them that he pulled along side them and rolled his window down and asked if they needed a ride some where. This was the Christian thing to do, of course, even for a Baptist. They accepted and opened the passenger door and both slid into the front seat with Lloyd sitting next to Wayne. They set their bags on the floorboard between their legs and Wayne continued down the road. He asked them how far they had to walk to and from the store and they told him about 12 miles or so each way. Shocked, Wayne asked, "You mean to tell me that you walk nearly 25 miles in the freezing cold to get groceries?" Kenny turned to look at Wayne dumbfounded and said, "Why, hell no, man! We wouldn't walk that far for groceries! We had to go get some hooch to get us through the weekend!" Wayne leaned forward and saw that the four paper grocery bags on the floor of his car were indeed filled with fifth-sized bottles of various liquors. Lloyd then leaned down and pulled out a fifth of whiskey that had already been opened and took a big swig. He then leaned into Wayne and asked, "Hey buddy! You want a slug off this?

As Wayne told me this, I was laughing my ass off. I finally looked at Wayne and devilishly asked, "Well, did you do the hospitable thing and take a nip?"

Wayne just rolled his eyes and grinned. "Nope! I was tempted but I really didn't want to put my lips to the same bottle that this old boy had been slobbering on!"

Wayne took the Maddox brothers home that day and vowed that he would never pick them up again. He said if they were that determined to tie one on, then he'd just let the Good Lord get them home on their own two feet. And besides, his car now smelled like cheap hooch. He said the old ladies in his congregation were already suspicious of his long hair and magic act. He surely didn't need to be seen riding around with the Maddox brothers in his car!

Sadly, Wayne and Donna moved away from our neighborhood a few years later. He received a new preaching assignment up near Mitchell, Indiana. Just as quickly as they had come into our lives, they were gone. Oh, my mother tried to keep in contact with them, but eventually, she just lost touch. I often wonder about Wayne and perhaps one day, I'll try to look him up. We have many new neighbors since then, some have stayed and some have moved on; however, in the short time that he was a part of our lives, Wayne Haun, the long-haired, magician-preacher taught me a valuable lesson about life: Religion doesn't make the preacher or the man. Only God can work that magic!

Mr. Hornickel's Room

Working as a school teacher in a large, urban high school allows me to venture into a vastly different cultural setting than the one in which I was raised and still live in. Each day, I walk the halls of a place that is so far removed from the country world that I am used to. It is a place that is racially, ethnically, and culturally diverse situated in a highly urban surrounding. The closest thing to an agriculture class is the conservation club, which consists of a handful of students who plant trees on Arbor Day, mulch the flower beds in front of the school, and raise a few Poinsettias in the school's small hothouse to sell at Christmas time. My students listen with awe when they hear me talk about owning horses, raising cattle, and driving tractors. Most of my fellow teachers are themselves urbanites that were either raised in the city or left the farm for good when they headed off to college so many years ago. I am not totally alone. There are a few others in the school who live in the country; however, I am the only one who truly lives on an operational farm where crops are grown, livestock is raised, and tractors are driven.

By now, most of my colleagues know that I am a bona fide, honest-to-goodness, hay-baling, tractor-driving, manure-shoveling, corn-growing, cattle-raising, overall-wearing, clod-hopping, farmer-at-heart, live-in-the-sticks, country boy. Some even have me on speed dial whenever they need an answer to a question on agriculture or country heritage.

[*Ring-ring-ring*] "Mr. Hornickel's room. What? What is *head cheese*? Why, it is the farm equivalent to waste not; want not! Seriously, it is a processed meat product made by cooking down the heads and scrap meat of slaughtered hogs. Excuse me? What was that retching sound? Hello?"

[*Ring-ring-ring*] "Mr. Hornickel's room. What are *Prairie Oysters*? Hmmm...Uhmm...Well, the fried testicles of young bull calves. Yes, you have to remove them from the calf before you fry them. No, I am not making this up! Yes, they are edible...No, I don't eat them...Sorry I grossed you out...but you asked!"

[*Ring-ring-ring*] "Mr. Hornickel's room. How much does a new

John Deere combine cost? Oh, somewhere around 300,000 dollars. No. 300 *thousand* dollars...No! A thousand dollars times 300! No, I am not pulling your leg! Yes, I am aware that is a lot of money! Yes, I know that is more than what you probably paid for your house. Welcome to *my* world!"

[*Ring-ring-ring*] "Mr. Hornickel's room. Are there really ghosts of dead baseball players in corn fields? No, coach, I have yet to see Shoeless Joe Jackson in my corn field. And no, I have never heard anyone whisper, 'If you build it, he will come,' while standing out in the corn. What? Well...it is because it was a movie! It was a made-up story. No, I am not laughing at you, I swear!"

While my colleagues have grown used to my country-boy farm background, they still have difficulty understanding that most of us country folks don't live life in the same lane as the urbanite city folks do. For example, every year around the first of February, someone will ask me if we are planning a big Super Bowl party. Of course, my answer is "Nope. Don't watch the Super Bowl." This usually baffles them as they cannot understand why we wouldn't throw a party to celebrate a sport that they believe originated in the country; after all, they play football in Alabama and Texas and everyone knows that Alabama and Texas is filled with rednecks and cowboys. While I am at it, let me set the record straight; we don't throw Daytona 500 or Indy 500 parties, nor do we have a National Tractor Pull Finals party or a Professional Bull Riding Championship party. It is true that I watch the NCAA Men's Basketball Tournament but I am a Hoosier and live in Indiana. It is a state law for everyone to watch basketball or face possible prosecution. And just because we own horses doesn't mean that we go crazy every spring and throw a three-day party to celebrate the Kentucky Derby!

Of course, someone will usually make a snide comment about us country folks not being sophisticated enough to appreciate the finer things in life like cheese balls made in the shape of footballs, eating hot wings doused in red hot sauce, and drinking beer while watching a bunch of over-paid, ill-behaved, professional athletes; a barrage of ridiculous commercials; and lip-synced halftime shows filled with wardrobe malfunctions. My response to all of that is always the same: Our lack of interest in all of these over-commercialized sports celebrations has nothing to do with our lack of sophistication and culture; it has more to do with the fact that we farm folks are usually too busy working to have a party just for the sake of having a party. If that makes us dull or boring, then so be it.

The reality is that most people who live in the city don't seem to understand that there is a difference between living in the country and being a farmer. The country is filled with people who aren't farmers, much to the chagrin of most farmers. The purchase of a patio home on three acres and a John Deere riding mower from The Home Depot doesn't make one a farmer. For the record, mowing a two-acre lawn and planting petunias in the flower bed isn't equivalent to cutting twelve acres of fescue and alfalfa hay and planting a hundred acres of corn. Farming is a profession where the point of the endeavor is to turn a profit (hopefully) and grow a business within the confines of an established lifestyle. Living in the country is simply the act of residing in a rural setting.

Now, I don't have a thing in this world against people who only reside in the country. I don't blame them for wanting to get away from the congestion and restriction of urban life. After all, I was raised out here and I know just how peaceful and serene the country is. I just want them to understand that this is the country and we want to keep it that way. If we wanted to live in the city, we'd sell the cows and tractors and move on up to the east side, to a dee-luxe apartment in the sky. If the city folks move out here then they need to be prepared to adapt to the country; not change the country to resemble the city that they wanted to get away from in the first place.

What I generally tell all of my teacher friends at school is that the country isn't just the place where I live; it is my way of life. While we life-long farm dwellers make it look easy, country life is very complex and challenging. Take, for example, when a big winter snow storm hits. Country life demands that you are prepared for anything instead of living from storm-to-storm. Cows still have to be fed when there is a foot of snow on the ground or an inch of ice covering everything. Survival out here isn't as simple as stopping off at the Kroger and grabbing a gallon of milk, a loaf of bread, and then hibernating like a grizzly bear. If we are cut off from outside world, we have to be ready to survive on our own. Country living is based on a self-sufficiency that is automatic and reactionary rather than a dependency on others to solve the problems. If a massive snow makes the roads impassable to even the county snowplows, we country folk are ready to work around the clock with large farm tractors and bucket loaders to clear the roads to keep commerce open and life on a normal schedule.

Most of my teacher friends can't understand why I prefer this lifestyle; after all, it would be much easier to just *live* in the country instead of doing all of that farm work. It is true that farming isn't a get-rich occupation and the amount of labor required generally outweighs the financial returns. What they don't understand is that farming isn't just about making money; it is about living the rural American Dream. I like baling hay. I enjoy shoveling manure. Harvesting corn is fun. Operating those big tractors gives me a rush. Raising cattle is rewarding. Farming *is* hard work but it is fun, too. At times it is very, very tiring and sometimes it is dirty, but at the end of every arduous, filthy farm job is a feeling of satisfaction that you have participated in a small, yet significant way in feeding the world. Making money is great but the real reward is in the feeling that you are a part of the oldest organized profession in the world: farming.

There is, of course, one more benefit to the farming lifestyle. Farmers are independent, self-sufficient, there-is-nothing-I-can't-do, jack-of-all-trades, survivalists. On the front of the high school where I teach is the message: "Producing Learners for Life." That is true of the farming lifestyle, as well. Living the farm life makes you a life-time learner. Whenever farmers are faced with a new challenge, they gather their resources and they learn how to do whatever it is that they need to do to meet that new challenge. Sometimes, when I think about all of the things that I have learned in my 50 years of living the farm life, I am amazed.

One of my fellow teachers was having a problem with his riding lawn mower. He asked me, "Where do you take your lawn mower when it needs repairs?"

My answer: "No where. I do it myself."

He looked at me skeptically and said, "No, I mean when it needs to have the engine rebuilt or a broken part welded?"

Again, my response: "No where. I do it myself." He just shook his head and walked away. Perhaps he can find someone at his Super Bowl party who can fix his lawn mower.

Oh, I know that it appears that I am just criticizing those who weren't as fortunate as I to have been raised on a farm. Thomas Jefferson once wrote: *Everyone has to be born somewhere; blessed are those who were born to the farm, for the fate of the world is at their hands.* When I think about it in that context, living the farm life is a huge responsibility. After all, who do you think produced all of that food that is served during those Super Bowl parties? It is a dirty job, but someone has got to do it.

The Unsung Hero

The next time you sit down for big, hearty breakfast; take a moment to ponder how all of that food got on your plate and who was responsible for putting it there. Let's start with the juice in your glass. Before it was orange juice concentrate in a jug, it was an orange growing on a tree on a farm in Florida. And on that farm was a farmer who worked many, many hard hours in the Florida heat to make sure that you have juice in your glass. Yes, it is true that he was paid for that orange; but think of all he and his family had to go through to get his product from the tree to your table. The nights tending to the orchard heaters when a unseasonal frost threatened to ruin the crop; the days of mixing and spraying chemicals to keep insects from devastating the fruit; the long hours in the hot sun to make sure the oranges were picked and shipped to the processor on time; and the nights he had to wonder if the crop would bring enough to feed his family and allow him to continue his profession for another year. All of this so you can have a glass of juice with your breakfast.

Now, let's move to the bacon on your plate. It began on a family farm in Iowa when a litter of pigs were born in the middle of a cold night in January. Again, a farmer and his family were responsible for the many hours of working 18-hour days to make sure that the corn was grown and harvested; that the feed was blended properly using the best ingredients; that those pigs were kept healthy and clean to insure that they would yield the highest quality product. Don't forget the depression that the farmer felt when he read the reports that said the United States was importing pork from some South American country because it was cheaper; and the bitter satisfaction of receiving only a few dollars of profit per head when his product finally goes to market. All of this so you can have good-tasting bacon with your breakfast.

Before you take a drink of that glass of milk, think about the morning five days before when the farmer was up at 3:30 am to begin milking the cows to obtain the contents of your glass. Think long and hard about the hours of back-breaking work that he and his family put in baling hay in the summer heat. Take time to imagine what it is like to sell your product without knowing how much you'll receive because milk isn't traded on the stock market and isn't supported with a price guarantee, leaving him literally at the mercy of the wholesale buyers. Ask yourself how you would feel if you knew that there was a chance that you may have to sell the farm that had been in your family for over one hundred and fifty years because you had lost money producing milk for three straight years. Think about how all of this is done so you can have ice cold milk with your breakfast.

Take a look at those two eggs on your plate. Think of the labor that the farmer had to perform so you can have farm-fresh eggs that are free from harmful bacteria and diseases. The days and nights he spent working to make the feed, provide the water, and gather the eggs so that they would be shipped to the supplier clean and free from cracks and blemishes. The disappointment he felt when he realized that he barely made enough to pay his operating costs. The determination in his heart and mind when he continues to farm because it was what he was born to do and it is what he knows how to do best; or the doubt that he feels when he contemplates how he will send his son to college to find a new profession instead of teaching him how to help feed the world. All of this so you can farm-fresh eggs with your breakfast.

Now, look at that toast that is so neatly resting on the edge of your plate. It started out as a bag of seed wheat on a Kansas farm with a farmer and his family putting all of their heart and soul into their crop. The hours and hours of preparing the soil with $250,000 dollar tractors burning $3.75 diesel fuel; the prayers said each day for rain to make the crop grow without the devastation of harsh winds or hail; the long, endless days of harvesting the grain with massive combines that each cost as much as a luxury home in the suburbs; the disbelief over the dramatic drop in price at the exact time when the wheat must go to market; and the stabbing pain and anger felt when the farmer overhears the public blame him for the price of a loaf of bread. Then think of the nights when that farmer had to miss his son's basketball game or his daughter's choir recital because the weather was threatening and he had to work in the fields. And don't forget to thank his wife for working a twelve-hour shift as a nurse at the local hospital so her family can continue to farm and produce the wheat that is used to make the bread that now sits as toast on your plate.

And when you are tempted to complain that this breakfast cost you over six dollars, remember that the true unsung heroes of our world are the farmers who received less than fifty cents of those six dollars that you just spent on a healthy, nutritious, life-sustaining breakfast. When you drive down the road and look over at a farmer working the fields in his big, air conditioned tractor and contemplate that it must be nice to work in such comfort, think about what goes on outside of that tractor each and everyday so that we can eat better than any other nation in the world. We Americans are truly spoiled when it comes to our food supply because most of us never consider where our food comes from. Farming is one of the most back-breaking and stressful occupations in today's modern economy, one that most Americans would not and could not perform. We are the best fed nation in the world and we owe it all to a small but proud group of dedicated individuals who accept the responsibility of not only feeding America, but the world.

Everything we do, everything we are, and everything we will become hinges upon those rapidly fading, un-sung heroes, the American Farmer.

The Real Mister Ed

I am always being asked by people if I saw this show or that show on the TV the previous night. And I always have to tell them that I don't watch TV anymore because I don't think there are any programs worth watching. Call me old fashion, but *Desperate Housewives* just can't measure up to *I Love Lucy* for pure entertainment value. If you disagree with that, well, then you just don't know good TV when you see it. At any rate, these modern TV shows are too explicit; they just don't leave anything for the imagination.

Of course, nothing prepared me for the day that one of my favorite TV shows from the past came to life right in our barn. When I was a young lad, I would watch with wide-eyed wonder each week as Mr. Ed, the talking horse would crack one-liners at his human side-kick, Wilbur. In my child mind, I never even considered that horses can't really talk; I guess I just figured that if it was on TV, then it must be real. Of course, *The Mister Ed Show* went off of the air and I grew up and that was the end of that. Or so I thought.

One day, many years later, my wife, Carolyn, purchased her first horse, a Golden Palomino yearling that she named Diamond. He was named this because of a small, white diamond patch on the tip of his muzzle. At first, Diamond was just like any other young horse. He was a bit skittish and not very social with people. As he matured, however, he began to develop a very human disposition which I attributed to Carolyn's method of training, Native American horse whispering. By the time he was three, Diamond had become a rural character in his own right. And of course we would laugh and call him "Mister Ed" because he had such a human-like personality. And then it happened.

I walked in the barn one day to feed the horses. Diamond was in his stall, waiting impatiently for his dinner when I noticed that he turned and put his rear up to the gate. As I started to walk past his stall, someone said, "Hey! How about giving me a scratch back there? I'd do it myself but I can't seem to reach my tail!" I stopped dead in my tracks and turned around. There wasn't anyone else in the barn with me. Well, great! I had been wondering at what age senility would begin to set in so I guess the time had finally arrived. I shook my head and started to walk on when the voice again rang out, "Hey, Wilbur. Are you deaf or something? I said I need a scratch back there!"

Slowly, I turned back to Diamond's stall and stared at the big, golden animal. "Diamond? Did you say something," I asked.

Diamond turned his head in my direction and said, "Well, it certainly wasn't the cat asking for his butt to be scratched! That would be stupid, wouldn't it?"

With total disbelief, I said, "I must be dreaming. Horses can't talk. This all some sort of dream."

Again, the voice rang out, "Wilbur, if you're dreaming, hurry and wake up and scratch my back side, will you? I am about to loose my mind in here!" I dropped the feed bucket that was in my hand and just stood there looking at Diamond. "I need to go get Carolyn. She is never going to believe this!" Before I could move, Diamond swung around in the stall and said, "Now, just hold your horses, Wilbur. There are some rules to this mental breakdown that you think you're having. First of all, Carolyn knows I can talk. Who do you think taught me that I could actually communicate with humans? Secondly, you're not hearing me with your ears; you're hearing me in your head, so this is just between you and me."

I reached down and grabbed my arm and pinched real hard to make sure that I wasn't taking a nap under a tree somewhere. No...this wasn't a dream. The horse continued on. "You need to understand that you and I are tuned in to the same mental frequency, so don't go blaming me if you're hearing me talk. I have been talking since the day I got here; you just haven't been listening...until now. I'm just an ordinary horse who, by the way, STILL NEEDS HIS BUTT SCRATCHED!"

Numbly, I reached through the gate and began scratching Diamond's backside. "You have no idea how good that feels, Wilbur. Now, be a chum and get me some sweet feed. I am feeling a bit light-headed." I filled the feed bucket and dumped into Diamond's feed container. He began eating and said, "Fanks eber so mush. Hey! I foud usf a frake of hay swhile you're grat it."

44

I looked at him and frowned. "Didn't anyone teach you some manners," I asked. "Don't talk with you mouth full! It's impolite." Diamond snorted and continued eating. I turned to the horse in the next stall. "Frankie, can you talk, too?" Frankie just looked at me and snorted.

"No, he can't talk, Wilbur...at least not to you," Diamond said. "After all, he is just a horse. Everyone knows that horses can't talk!"

I wheeled around toward Diamond's stall and exclaimed, "What do you mean? You're talking!"

"Exactly," he said. "And your point, Wilbur?"

I thought for a moment and then said, "I guess I don't have one. Oh, and by the way...why do you keep calling me Wilbur?"

Diamond snorted and then belched, "I don't know. Why don't you ask Eugene Gleitz?"

I looked at Diamond and shook my head. "How in the hell do you know Eugene Gleitz?"

Diamond snorted and replied, "Well, I don't but I have heard you speak of him from time-to-time. Oh, by the way...I think it is hilarious that he calls you Wilbur. It kind of fits, dontcha think?"

Okay, before you start thinking that old Uncle Bill is either ready for a stay in the Ha-Ha Hotel or that I am the biggest liar in Harrison County; let me assure that Diamond *can* talk. In fact, all horses have the ability to "talk" to us *if* you can open a line of communication with them. Equine psychologists have established that it is very probable that horses do have the ability to use telepathy to communicate with humans. So why can't all horses do this? It is because they haven't been taught the correct language in which to communicate in. Horse owners who spend a great deal of time with their animals and talk to them while they are working with them are, in fact, teaching them language. Horses can learn things rather quickly, in three seconds or less, in most cases. Once the horse learns our language, it is just a matter of developing a close enough relationship with the animal to open a line of telepathic communication.

Now, I know that some of you are reading this and are probably laughing and saying that this whole premise is just silly. My response is this: Believe what you want to believe. I know that Diamond and I do have real conversations. Maybe not like Wilbur and Mister Ed on that old TV show, but trust me, we do talk on a regular basis. Aunt Carolyn likes to say that a horse is just like big dog with a cat's attitude, which means that they are loyal and protective just like dogs, but very curious and highly intelligent like most cats. If you spend enough time around a horse and really get to know them on a personal level, you will discover that this is true. And if you are able to do this, then don't be surprised if one day you discover that you are able to "hear" the horse's thoughts just as plainly as if he were actually talking directly to you, because in reality, he is. Again, if you don't believe all of this, well, then just consider this one of my tall-tales or else that I am having a complete mental breakdown; both have been known to happen from time-to-time.

In addition to being able to talk, Diamond is also a highly educated. One afternoon while I was cleaning stalls, Diamond came up to the barn gate and said he needed to ask me some questions about Shakespeare. Diamond snorted and said, "The other horses and I were discussing the psychological aspects of *Hamlet* and I was curious why Shakespeare didn't just have young Hamlet directly confront Claudius instead of pretending to be mentally ill over his father's death?"

I looked up from the manure pile I was shoveling and stared at Diamond. "Are you kidding me," I asked, dumbfounded. "You and the other horses are actually discussing Shakespeare's *Hamlet?* Next, you're gonna tell me that you've actually read Shakespeare!"

Diamond shook his head and replied, "No, of course not! Horses can't read! Any dumbass knows that!" I leaned on the pitchfork and frowned. The last thing in this world I ever thought I'd be doing at 49 years of age is cleaning the stall of a talking horse with a smart mouth!

"Well, Mr. Smarty-Horse, if you haven't read Shakespeare, then how do you know the story of *Hamlet*," I asked.

Diamond looked at me and wrinkled his nose. "Well, Mr. English teacher, you have read *Hamlet* and since we are communicating telepathically, I am privy to all of your thoughts, including all of the stuff you have read. Kind of scary, isn't it?" Before I could respond to this new revelation, Diamond snorted and asked, "So why are you thinking about Carolyn taking a shower while you're shoveling manure?"

And it was then that I realized that telepathic communication with a horse can be downright embarrassing at times. So, right then and there, I had a very long discussion with Diamond about the birds and the bees. He listened intently without saying a word, occasionally raising his eyebrows and snorting at the really good parts. Once finished, I asked, "Now, do you understand why I prefer to think of Carolyn in that way when I am shoveling your crap? Do you have any more questions before I get back to work?"

Diamond shook his head and snorted. "Well, I am kind of curious about one thing, Wilbur. Why in the world would you explain all of that stuff to a *gelded* horse?" Well, I guess he had a very good point.

As I close, Diamond shared with me a joke that he thought you, the readers, might like:

Do you know why most horses can't drive cars? They are always stalled! Get it? *Stalled!* Well, I guess you just had to hear it from the horse's mouth.

Ralph's Mystery Theater

Like most farm boys, I grew up believing in my heart that my father was the bravest, most fearless man in the world. In all of my youth, I had never known him to be "afraid" or "scared" of anything. Of course, that didn't mean that he would just go out and throw caution to the wind and do stupid things; he generally always used good sense in situations where danger was imminent. But in regards to things unseen or imagined, I never knew dad to show fear. Now that I am an adult, I know that everyone has certain fears or apprehensions; that is a natural part of being human. But my dad was always one cool character in the face of the unknown...except one dark, spring night.

This was in the mid-1970's and like everyone else who raised crops in our part of the country that meant that every acre of ground had to be turned under to prepare the seedbed for spring planting. It was a Friday evening and my dad and I had fueled our big diesel John Deere tractors and headed to the farm acreage that we referred to as the "Rehoboth Place" because it was next to the Rehoboth Presbyterian Church. My grandfather had purchased this piece of property years before and it was located in a rather sparsely populated area of Harrison County, over on the next ridge from our home farm. Both tractors were big, open-platform machines with large fender-mounted AM radios to keep us company into the long, cool nights of field work.

Spring had come early that year and with it the rains that brought the new vegetation to life. By early May, the trees were turning green with leaves and everything was growing, including the weeds. I was perched up on the big 4320 John Deere with the radio blasting out the local AM rock station, WAKY, out of Louisville, Kentucky. Like most teens of the seventies, I was hooked on rock & roll. Despite my rural roots, country music was way too "twangy" for my taste; The Eagles were the closest thing to country that I listened to.

My dad, however, had his radio tuned to WHAS, an AM super-station also located in Louisville and had been listening to the Milton Metz radio call-in show. As the hours passed, the evening light faded into a cool, dark, star-filled night. At 11:00 pm, WAKY radio was required by FCC law to turn down its transmitter power and my music faded into a barely tolerable static. I reached over and changed the station to WHAS which hosted a syndicated show each Friday night out of New York called *The Radio Mystery Theater*. This was a throw-back to the old days of a radio theater production. *The Radio Mystery Theater's* tag line was "tales of mystery and suspense from the macabre." Even though I would have preferred to listen to rock and roll, I did enjoy a good mystery tale, so I settled in for the hour-long radio production.

My dad was a huge fan of *The Radio Mystery Theater*, in part because it reminded him of his childhood days of listening to radio theater broadcasts on the big family radio at home. I knew that he would be listening to the broadcast as well, and he had already fore-warned me that we were going to be working very late because he wanted to get the plowing finished on this particular acerage before the forecasted rain set in. I was prepared to stay in the field that night until at least 1:30 in the morning before returning home. With nothing else to do but navigate the big tractor through the field, I listened as the broadcast began.

The story that evening was about a scoundrel of a guy who was married to a rich, rather eccentric lady who was obsessed with her house plants. She was the heiress of a large estate that had been left to her by her wealthy parents and she had a large hothouse that was connected to the mansion in which they lived. As the plot unfolded, it was revealed that he thought that she was crazy because she would go into the hothouse and spend hour after hour talking to all of her exotic plants. She even named them and began calling them "her friends." Her obsession with her plants had driven him to have an affair with another woman and they soon hatched a devious plan to kill his eccentric wife. Then he could inherit all of her wealth, marry his mistress, and they could live happily ever after, with all of her money, of course.

At this point in the story, I was on the edge of my tractor seat and was waiting for the plot to unfold. Across the field in the darkness, my dad was also intently listening, though I didn't know at the time that he was thinking that this story was a bit over dramatic and corny. Me? I was hooked!

The guy and his girlfriend decided that best time to kill his kooky wife was during a big party that had been planned at the mansion. The wife, who was an extreme introvert and didn't like big crowds, escaped from the party guests to her greenhouse to spend time with her only true friends, her plants. While she was there, the husband slipped in and hit her in the back of the head with a shovel amidst all of her exotic plants and vines. He then cleverly framed the bitter old family gardener with the crime and everything looked to be going in his favor.

I was really into this production by now, just waiting for the plot twist that would move this story from an ordinary murder mystery to a weird, spooky tale. *Back to the story.*

A few days after the wife's funeral, the husband was preparing to move his new sweetheart into the mansion so they could live happily ever after. He and his mistress-turned-fiancée were having a conversation about their new life together while standing in the greenhouse. They both agreed that the plants and greenhouse must go; its location would make a great place for a new pool and patio. The guy told his mistress that she should leave before any of the servants got suspicious and began to put two and two together. So she departed and left him there in the green house alone.

I was at the opposite end of the field from my dad, who was beginning to plow along the edge of the field next to the woods. In the distance I could see his tractor lights and could barely make out his shape on the tractor in the cool darkness. And then the plot twist came without warning. I heard a scream in the night and was startled because I wasn't absolutely sure that it had come from the radio. It sounded like it had come from across the field. The plants in the greenhouse, having been witness to the man's devious crime, reached out and grabbed the man by the neck, entangling him with vines. As the man struggled, the plants extracted their revenge for killing their friend, his now deceased wife.

At that same exact moment, fantasy had suddenly become reality as a huge, wild grapevine hanging down from a tree along the field's edge snared my dad's neck and began choking him as the radio theater production played on.

I looked across the field and could see my dad. He had abruptly stopped the tractor and was struggling up on the operator's platform. By the time I had got to the end of the field where he was at, he had finally turned the tractor out into the plowed field. I pulled up next to him and asked what was wrong. He yelled back over the big diesel engines in a loud, shaky voice that "a damned grapevine had just tried to kill him" and began heading for the road, motioning for me to follow. As we headed across the field toward the county road, the Radio Mystery Theater broadcast came to an end with its unsettling tagline: *"Join us again next week for another chilling tale from the macabre."* At that moment, the hair stood up on my neck.

Did that grapevine really reach out and try to kill my dad, or was it just a quirky coincidence? I guess we'll never know for certain, but it sure did get my dad's attention and that was certainly enough for me. I do know one thing for certain: That was the last time my dad ever had thoughts about a *Radio Mystery Theater* production being corny. Sometimes livin' country can be a little spooky!

High-Tech Redneck

Okay, I'll admit it right now. I stole the title for this chapter from an early 90's country music hit by George Jones, which now makes me laugh for a couple of reasons. First, I have never really considered myself a George Jones music aficionado; not that there is anything wrong with George Jones' music but he just never really got my blood pumping. I am more of an Alabama/ Travis Tritt/ Vince Gill type of country music fan. I guess it goes back to my early musical roots that consisted of a bizarre mixture of Elvis Presley, Johnny Cash, The Beatles, and The Rolling Stones. Hey, I grew up during the 1970's. After listening to a decade of progressive album rock, a bit of disco, and early electronic high-tech music, I just couldn't get into that twang-thang. If you happen to be a George Jones fan, then more power to you.

No, the real reason for my amusement on this point is because of all people in this world to make a relevant statement about modern rural lifestyle, who would have guessed that it would be George Jones? After four decades of songs about drinkin' and cheatin' and more drinkin' and even more drinkin', I would have had my doubts that he would hit the charts with a song that made a relevant point about country life and the new age of technology. Forget the fact that he recorded this song in the early 1990's when high-tech was a cell phone the relative size and weight of a brick and videos were still being produced on VHS tape. To coin the old phrase: "We have come a long way, baby!"

Once upon a time in rural America, most country folks were content to stay at least 20 years behind the urban world when it came to technology and high-tech gadgetry. For example, in the late 1960's, when most urban dwellers were rushing out to purchase the new-fangled color TV's, the folks out here in the country were just getting used to watching soap operas and the six o'clock news in black and white. Most rural households didn't make the switch to color TV for at least 10 to 15 years after the rest of the world had been watching Walter Cronkite in full, living color. Some may be quick to point out that some country folks didn't have the extra money to spend on this new age technology, but that really wasn't the reason. The real reason was need: what possible difference did it make if the *Gunsmoke* was in color or black and white?

I can remember when we got our first color TV. It was in the spring of 1969 when my mom and dad went to Conrad's Appliance Store in Corydon and plopped down close to 250 dollars for a 19-inch diagonal console, color TV. The old 15-inch black and white, table-top Philco was retired to the attic where it remains to this very day. No kidding. That old two-tone green Philco is still in the attic in our old home place where my sister now resides. Someday, when I finally get around to building a rural heritage museum here on our farm, I will venture into that old attic and retrieve that old high-tech relic from my childhood and put it on display for all to see. That or I'll use it for a boat anchor because that old table-top TV must weigh at least a hundred pounds!

One of the reasons that my dad was so quick to make the switch to color TV was because America was getting close to landing a man on the moon and he wanted to make sure that we could witness that historic moment in color. And then, just a few months after he purchased that new color TV, we all sat around in the living room and watched Neil Armstrong and Buzz Aldrin take man's first steps on the moon.

Of course, the big surprise was that NASA didn't have the room on board the spacecraft for a color TV camera, so the whole thing was broadcast in black and white. Oh well…at least Walter Cronkite looked good in color as he rubbed his hands together and giggled like a school girl when the historic moment arrived. Come to think of it, that whole moon landing event didn't go real well in terms of color TV. Apollo 11 only took a black and white camera; Apollo 12's color camera broke and no one got to see anything; and then Apollo 13 had a bit of bad luck and didn't land on the moon at all, so it was well over a year before we got to see the moon in color. And what a surprise! The moon was pretty much all black and white!

Most of rural America's experience with the world of high technology was centered on the TV for the better part of twenty years. By the end of the 70's, when most of our urban neighbors had cable TV and could chose from a wide selection of channels, we farm folk were still happy to have three channels of network TV, one independent station that played 30 year old re-runs, and one public broadcast station to give us culture and keep us informed. And if the president was on, you were screwed because he was on every channel, which to me didn't make any sense. Why would all of the major networks carry the same program? So we country folks watched and listened to the president even though no president after Carter ever mentioned farm policy in a nation-wide address. The city folks watched HBO instead of our fearless leaders while we country-folk had to watch even though it was apparent that modern presidents didn't even believe that we existed anymore. Ah, life down on the farm!

Now, let's fast-forward to today. The average modern farmer of the 21st century is more high tech than his urban neighbors ever dreamed of being. Nearly every farmer and rural redneck has a cell phone with Internet capability and texting features. Look inside of a modern farm vehicle (pickup truck) and you'll likely find a satellite navigation system, most with real-time data uplink and voice command. A majority of all new farm trucks and tractors come standard with satellite digital radio and some even have video download capability to get repair information in the field and even order parts via a web link. Most combines utilize a Global Positioning Satellite system (GPS) and have on-board computers that calculate yield ratios, grain moisture, and create yield maps of the field to insure proper plant food application for the next crop year. Farmers can even track the weather with a real-time Doppler radar link via the GPS satellite. Kind of makes the city folks' IPad look puny, doesn't it?

Most large livestock operations are controlled totally by computer systems. The large-market hog farms use computerized feeding systems to insure that every animal is receiving the correct amount of the needed nutrients to insure proper growth and maximum efficiency. Many modern farm boys (and girls) find themselves toting a laptop computer with them into the barn so that they can have a direct link to the markets so they can sell their goods at the exact moment when the prices are at their highest.

Talk about being connected!

None of this high-tech country wizardry is surprising when you consider that farming has become a technology-driven industry that survives on extremely slim profit margins where even a penny or two of profit gain can make a huge difference in the overall bottom line for the 21st century farmer. Farming is a business, after all, and the name of the game in business is to maximize efficiency and make money. A laptop computer or a GPS system is now just another piece of farm machinery like a tractor or a combine. These are all just tools of the agribusiness trade.

This high-tech country gadgetry isn't just confined to the farm. Rural redneck activities like deer and turkey hunting have gone high-tech as well. The days of walking out into the woods with a gun and sitting in the cold until a deer shows up are long gone. Now, thanks to Bass Pro Shops, deer hunters can hit the woods wired up like the space shuttle. They have digital tree cams and infrared tracking systems to help them locate their prey and maximize their chances of bagging the "big one." Holy crap! These guys have the trees wired for sound and video, their guns equipped with laser sights, and an IPhone with a Blue Tooth link and GPS tracking to help them stay in constant contact with the other high-tech Jethros who are in on the hunt. And the turkey hunters aren't using an old fashion scratch box call anymore. Why would they? They now can use digitally recorded turkey mating sounds played back through Bose micro sound systems to reproduce turkey sounds that could fool even the most discerning gobbler. Of course, these systems *are* illegal but you know what they say: All's fair in love and hunting!

Of course, most of this redneck gadgetry got its start several years ago with a device that revolutionized the art of fishing. I am speaking of the technological wonder known as the Hummingbird Depth Finder, which was developed by a Fishing Technologist from Arkansas by the name of Tom Mann. It does scare me a bit to know that there are actually people out there who are referred to as "fishing technologists."

Mann decided that what every fisherman needed on his boat besides a cooler full of Budweiser and a case of beef jerky was a device that could "see" beneath the surface of the water and into its murky depths to find the fish. His theory was simple: Why fish in a place where the fish aren't? So, he developed a sonar device that could locate schools of fish and direct the sportsman in the boat to the exact area where the fish were. To some, this sounds like a joke. To date over 1 million Hummingbirds have been sold, allowing Mann to build a fishing research institute in Alabama known as Fish World. Only in America!

To fully understand how the country became so technologically advanced, one most only look at the behavioral tendencies of the average, rural redneck. Typically, everything that they do, they do to the extreme. That is what makes them rednecks in the first place. Jeff Foxworthy describes the state of being a redneck as the glorious lack of sophistication. Translated, that means that most rednecks are rednecks because they don't know any better. When the new age of technology finally arrived in the country, we country folk were just so fascinated and intrigued by these high-tech gadgets, well, we just couldn't help ourselves. We were just like a bunch of kids gone wild in a Toys R Us store.

When I was a kid, we had a pen of hogs that got to biting on each other's tails. Now, hogs are omnivores. They'll eat anything, including each other! Well, after several hogs died from this brutal sort of cannibalistic play, my dad started trying all sorts of things to get those pigs to stop eating one another. Someone told him to put an old tire in the pen to act as a jumbo pacifier. Of course, every day one hog would manage to get himself stuck in the tire and we would have to wrestle him to the ground and pry it off.

Someone else suggested taking Jemison weed and cooking it down to make a sticky syrup to paint on their tails to keep them from chewing. The theory behind this (pardon the pun) was that Jemison weed is so bitter and distasteful that no hog in its right mind would want to chew on his neighbors ass-end after it had been coated with this stuff. All it ended up doing was stink up the house when dad cooked up a batch on mom's kitchen stove.

He was just about to give up when someone suggested putting empty soda cans in the pen. Dad was skeptical but figured what could it hurt? After all, we were losing two pigs a day, which was money lost. He gathered up a bag of cans and dumped them in the pen. Low and behold…it worked! Those pigs spent their days and nights just rooting those cans around and making quite a racket but by golly, it worked. It seemed that the pigs were so fascinated by the shiny cans and the noise that they could make with them, that they plumb forgot about eating each other.

When it comes to new high-tech gadgets, most redneck country folks are just like that pen of pigs. Giving an Android phone to a redneck is like giving a pig a can to play with. They'll shake it around and drool on for hours!

There is nothing more endearing than a typical country boy bouncing down the road in his pickup truck with his GPS a chirpin', his IPod docked in his digital sound system a blastin' out *Free Bird,* textin' with one hand, and web surfin' with the other. Who is driving the truck? Who the hell knows? It could be on a GPS Auto Trac for all we know. Yeah, Baby! You'd better watch out for those high-tech rednecks!

Livin' and Lovin' Country

I suppose by now you have guessed that I am a bit biased when it comes to living in the country. I make no apologies here; I was born in the country and I'll stay in the country till the day that I am laid beneath that good, old country soil forever. I am asked all of the time if I like living in the country and I always say, "No...I *love* living in the country!" And while we're on the subject of love, let me tell you: Country living is all about love.

There is nothing more romantic than watching a summer sun set on a country horizon, with a multitude of purples, oranges, and blues, all streaming together into a mixed pallet of brilliant color while faint stars begin to twinkle in the deep violet sky straight above as you sit there with your one special person at your side. As the last glimmer of light finally fades from view, a brilliant, glowing, neon-white moon begins its slow climb into the velvet blackness of a peaceful, night sky, bathing everything underneath a dreamy moon-glow as millions of crickets play a symphony of sound. Just as the summer moon reaches its apex in the stillness of the night, a faint breeze gently whispers and stirs, carrying on it the sweet nectar aroma of honeysuckle and corn flower as fireflies dance a wild ballet of phosphorescent green across the twilight landscape. That, my friends, is a romantic summer night in the country.

Or, how about a warm, late-fall afternoon, with a swirl of blazing colors gently rustling in the trees while squirrels dash about gathering nuts for the coming winter? The gentle rustling of a field of golden corn waiting to be harvested stirs as the smell of ripened persimmons and orange Osage mixes with the tingling hint of the coming frost. Walking together, hand-in-hand, down a well-worn, wooded path that leads to nowhere, you stop to take in the beauty of this moment before the cold, harsh winds of winter come and erase all evidence of this wistfully perfect fall day. Nothing stirs a lover's heart like an idyllic country autumn.

Perhaps it is the silent, stillness of a mid-winter snowfall as it covers the countryside with a thick blanket of cottony white, frozen powder. As you stand close, sharing warmth with someone special, the soundless silence of this majestic moment surrounds the two of you like a thick cloud. The smell of crisp cedar and pine, accented by the cold iciness, fills your nostrils as you gaze into each other's eyes, feeling the warmth of each other's love. Even the cold chill of a country winter cannot freeze the passion of two country lovers.

Of course, nothing is more romantic than spring, with its re-birth of nature and the formerly frozen world. The sound of birds chirping in lightly green trees as a gentle breeze blows life back into bright, sunny sky. The fertile smell of newly planted fields and the bawling of a baby calf somewhere in the distance surrounds you and that special someone as you lie on your backs in new grass, staring up into the brilliant blue sky of a warm spring afternoon. The sweet hint of spring flowers blooming accents the freshness of the country air that the two of you breathe, cleansing the cold, lifeless winter from your bodies. Spring in the country; could love find a more perfect place to grow?

Nothing can stir the emotions of love quite like the uninhibited freeness of the country with its purity and innocence. The sharing of love between two souls in the midst of the unspoiled country is the ultimate of the human experience for here we can truly find oneness within mother earth and all her glories. The union of heart, soul, and spirit is nurtured by the unscathed beauty of a world that is natural and pure. It is in the wide-open expanse of what we call "country" where two can truly become one, leaving behind the tangling confusion of the developed, mechanized, high-tech world.

I know that in the twenty-first century the experiences that I have just detailed are rare. With every minute that passes, another portion of the untamed, untouched countryside is forever lost to the movement we call progress. Concrete flows outward in the name of urban development like cold lava from an exploding mountain of technology and modernization. It cannot be helped; it is the nature of man to move outward and build. But no, this isn't about saving the country, or the world, or even the planet. This is about the purity and preservation of two things that I believe in: life in the country and love.

I do believe in livin' country; after all, the country is where I was born. It is my home. It is where I learned everything about life and how to survive. It is the place where I discovered my own soul, found out who and what I am, and became a spiritual being. And it is here in the country where I discovered that God truly does exist in the details of our world. He is all around me. He is *in* me. I also believe in love. Of all of the human emotions and experiences, love is the most powerful and beautiful. It is what we were created from and what we were born to do.

The one question that nearly every human ponders at some point in his or her existence in this world is the "why" question: *Why am I here?* It is my belief that we are here to love and be loved. Nothing more; nothing less. Again, if God is truly found in every detail of this world, including us, then we are living, breathing elements of Him: pure love.

For those who are lucky enough to live in the country, take time to share it with someone special, for just as corn grows in rich soil, so can love when it is shared under a country sky.

Two hearts intertwined in the midst of a field of hay,
And became one within the innocence of a country day.
Like the corn growing in the valley nearby,
Love grows in the blink of an eye.

Yes, the country is truly all about love. Don't take my word for it; experience it for yourself. There is nothing like love in the country.

Uncle Bill Hornickel

A Christmas in the Toilet

As the title suggests, this isn't your normal warm and fuzzy Christmas story. However, every word is true. With that said, let me take you back to 1984 when my family learned just how dedicated we were to the celebration of Christmas.

The holiday season had finally rolled around that year and as usual, my mom had busied herself with getting ready for Christmas day when all of the family would gather together at our house. The week before Christmas saw the tree go up in the living room, table decorations set out, a basket of nuts placed on the end table, and snacks and sweets of every manner and description filling the kitchen. Then, a day or two before Christmas Eve, mom would make her final journey to the grocery and pack the refrigerator so full of food that you almost had to use your shoulder to get the door closed. The house was cleaned one last time, the gifts were all wrapped and piled under the tree, and all of the pre-cooking was completed. Then finally, on the evening of December 24th, everything was ready for the "big day."

1984 represented a new experience for me for I had just become engaged to my first wife and would be spending Christmas Eve with her family that year. At noon on Christmas Eve, I showered and dressed, bid everyone a good-bye, and left for my future in-laws house over in a nearby town. As I pulled out of the farm driveway that afternoon, I was saddened by the prospect of not being at home on Christmas Eve. But, I rationalized, that is how life is when you become an adult; sometimes you have to leave the old ways behind you and move ahead.

Around 1:00 a.m. on the morning of Christmas, I returned home. It had been a very long day and I was tired; all I had on my mind was slipping into my bed and letting visions of sugar plums and all that stuff dance in my head while I drifted off into a peaceful sleep. I knew that everyone was surely in bed by now as was the custom in my family, especially on Christmas Eve. But as I pulled into the long driveway leading to our farm, I was startled to the see every light in the house on. My heart leapt into my throat;

61

something was wrong. My mind began racing...my God, what if someone was sick...or worse. What if someone had...died! What a minute! If something like that had happened they would have surely called me. By the time I had dismissed these silly notions, I was pulling my car into my usual parking spot by the garage. Well, there was only one way to find out what was going on; I had to go in.

I walked up to the back door, took a deep breath, and opened the door and stepped inside. I quickly surveyed the scene. Everything seemed normal, no wait...the tan vinyl floor was covered with a black, smudgy residue...and what is that smell? Oh no! That smells like...like sewage!

At that moment, my mother appeared at the end of the hallway leading from the bathroom. She was wearing a pair of old knit slacks, an old blouse, and blue fuzzy house slippers. Her hair was a mess and she looked as if she had been thrown on a rack and beaten. Her face displayed a despair that seemed to indicate that the end of the world had begun somewhere in our house. What fascinated me most were her house slippers which were covered with black, gooey, ooze that made them slightly reminiscent to a road-killed possum. She didn't speak. She just looked at me with a distant, sorrowful look and then retreated back down the hall like a wounded animal, leaving me to stand there in my confusion.

Well, there was only one way I was going to find what in the hell was going on and that was to investigate. By deductive reasoning I concluded that if there was an odor of sewage in the air then the most likely place to begin would be the bathroom. Just call me Sherlock Holmes. I slowly headed down the short hall to the bathroom. As I entered, I confronted a surreal scene that is difficult to describe; words cannot do justice to the menagerie of activity and mayhem contained within that small room.

My sister, Julie, was kneeling in the bathtub. Her arms and hands were coated with a blackish slime, her face had smudges of gray and black dotted about, and her hair was in disarray. She had the appearance of someone who had been dragged behind a car through a half dozen mud holes. Her face was painted with a look of despair similar to my mother's as she looked at me with eyes that pleaded only one request: "Help!"

Kneeling next to the toilet was Greg Mills, a local squirrel who had taken up residence at our farm. Greg was 19 and a member of the Army National Guard, an affiliation he took seriously as was evident in his attire. At about a hundred pounds, soaking wet, Greg was a wiry fellow who always seemed as if he had something to prove. He approached everything with a level of passion and bravado that was inspiring while at the same time just short of ridiculous. He was kind of a three-way cross between Rambo, Gilligan, and Barney Fife, all rolled up in a tight little bundle of nerves and expression. He was decked in army fatigue pants, combat service boots, and a brown, army tee-shirt. He was wearing a camo green field cap, turned around backwards with the bill sticking back and down toward his neck. From his neck dangled a set of dog tags, which he never took off in case he was killed in action. In action of what, I have no clue.

Greg's right hand was plunged deep into the toilet bowl with a garden hose that's end had apparently been tightly wrapped with old rags, creating a ball that would fit neatly into the large drain hole. The hose snaked back out of the bathroom and into the laundry room, where presumably it was hooked to the laundry sink. He looked up at me, peering through the gold wire-frame glasses that were perched upon his nose and said with set-jaw seriousness, "The shitter's plugged."

"Wow. And all this time I thought you guys were just trying to liven things up on Christmas Eve in my absence," I dead-panned. No one laughed. From the pit of my stomach crept the realization that I wasn't going to get to bed anytime soon.

My mother came shuffling back into the bathroom and took her place at the sink basin, were she proceeded to stuff an assortment of rags and a rubber surgical glove into the drain hole. My sister, as if silently cued, leaned down in the tub and began holding a soggy washcloth over the tub drain. At that moment, Greg yelled out, "Okay, turn her on!" I stood in quiet wonder as the hose swelled and squiggled slightly from the increasing water pressure. Apparently, my dad was operating the sink valve from the laundry room. As the pressure increased, a hissing sound began emanating from first the toilet and then the tub drain. It suddenly occurred to me that they were attempting to use water pressure to blow some massive clog from the main sewage drain. How ingenious... how inventive...how stupid! I nervously backed up against the wall. Still dressed in slacks, a sweater, and loafers, I was not properly attired for this type of entertainment. A minute passed...the hissing sound had increased to a sizzling and then, without warning, blackish water came shooting from under the washcloth that my sister was holding over the tub drain. Julie fought to hold the rag down to no avail; the pressurized water had found the easiest path of resistance and rag slipped from under her fingers, sending a fountain of black, foul sewage water erupting from the drain and into the face of my sister who screamed out an agonizing exclamation.

"Son-of-a-bitch! Shut it off!" yelled Greg, shaking his head in grim disappointment as he peered down into the toilet bowl, deep in thought. I looked at Julie but had to turn away. She was still kneeling in the tub amid the foul, black water as she looked up at me. A big drip of black slim hung at the end of her nose, like a foul wart. I fought the urge to laugh and was just about to lose the fight when my dad appeared in the bathroom. "What happened," he barked. "Well, it blew back through the tub drain," Greg said, implicating Julie for the failure of the grand plan.

"You're really gonna have to put some pressure down on that rag," Dad barked at Julie. He then turned to me and growled, "What the hell are you doing? You gonna just stand around or are you gonna help?" Well, that certainly was direct. I excused myself to go change, wondering if I could just slip out the door and make a get-a-way before anyone could catch me. Well, of course, I didn't and within a few minutes, I returned, dressed for battle against the dreaded evil that was our toilet; a friendly place of comfort that was now the enemy.

In my brief absence, the decision was made to take the toilet up from the floor and put the hose directly into the drain hole. Within a few minutes and several spewing outbursts of profanity, the toilet was unbolted from its moorings and carried outside to sit alone in the freezing night on our back step. The hose was rewrapped and threaded down the large gapping drain hole in the floor. The sink and tub drains were again sealed off under the hands of my mother and sister. The water pressure was applied and we waited…one minute…then two…we all began to get nervously confident. Greg looked at me and said, "By damn, I think we've got it!" My dad left his station at the laundry sink and came into the bathroom. "Well? Is it taking water," he asked.

Call me the pessimist but I had my doubts; I wasn't ready to claim victory just yet. "I don't know," I said hesitantly. "There seems to be a great deal of back pressure for a four inch drain."

My dad looked at me and asked, "Well, then where is the water going?"

I gave the question a moment of thought and then offered a theory. "You don't suppose the water is going up the vent pipe and onto the roof, do you?"

My dad's eyes widened in dumb-founded stare; he turned to my mother and said, "Helen, I need a flashlight!" She looked at him and then at the sink drain where her hands were pressing down on a rag. I jumped up and quickly took over for her at the sink so she could retrieve a flashlight for dad.

She shuffled off into the living room and returned a few moments later with a wrapped Christmas gift which she thrust at dad and said, "Here! It is one of your Christmas gifts. Go ahead and open it."

My dad just exploded. "I don't have time to open any damned Christmas gift. I need a flashlight! You open it!" My mom started to carefully remove the wrapping from the flashlight, taking her time as to not damage the contents. My dad's impatience was building exponentially and he finally exclaimed, "Hurry up every chance you get! We may have sewer water going down into the cistern right now!" The flashlight-gift was finally unwrapped and the batteries loaded in. Dad ran out the door and then returned to report that the water was definitely not coming up the vent pipe. Just as he returned to the bathroom, the old familiar sound of hissing and sizzling began emitting from the tub and sink drains. I put all of my weight down on the rag in the sink but eventually, I lost the battle; slimy, smelly water began erupting from the sink.

Dad ran to the laundry sink and shut the water off. Okay, a
setback; but we weren't ready to give up, not by a long-shot.

For the next hour, we waged war on that toilet. My dad was the
gritty, old field commander and we were his troops; forging ahead
against impossible odds with fierce determination. We would rally
and siege forward, using any and every possible idea, no matter
how extreme or obscure. But as the hour of three a.m.
approached, we began to smell defeat (*sorry, I just had to throw
that pun in there*); finally, my dad decided that it was time to take it
on the chin and wave the white flag of surrender. We had tried
every tool in our arsenal and still that toilet drain refused to take
liquid. Mercifully, the battle ended. We had lost the war.

Dad walked back into the bathroom and for a moment, we
were all silent, no one daring to speak or look at one another. We
had fought the good fight, but it was over; there would be no
functioning toilet in our house on Christmas Day. My mother stood
at the bathroom sink with her back to us, her head hung low and
her shoulders drooping. She didn't say anything at first; she only
sniffled a couple of times and then quietly said, "Well, I guess I'll
have to call everyone in the morning and let them know that
Christmas is canceled. We can't possibly have all of these people
over here with no bathroom!"

That's right, mom...let's cancel Christmas...over a toilet! No
sir-ee! We Hornickels are going to forge on and have the hap-hap
happiest Christmas since Bing Crosby danced with Danny freaking
Kaye (*Sorry. I had to throw a movie line in here somewhere*)!
Slowly, we rallied once more and began to clean up the slimy
mess that covered the bathroom and hallway of the house. We
mopped and scrubbed the floors, cleaned and disinfected the sink
and tub, and removed every trace of the toilet trauma from sight.

Greg and I made a quick trip out to my camper and retrieved
the Port-A-Pot, which we placed in the bathroom right over the
spot where the white porcelain commode had once proudly stood.
By 3:45, we had everything back to normal; well, as normal as it
was going to get. Our last act was to remove our foul-smelling
clothes and place them in a plastic bag which was taken out to the
farm shop. With that completed, we were finally able to drift off to

our beds, close our eyes, and slip into a winter slumber.

When morning finally came, each of us slipped off to either grandma's or Uncle Clarence's to grab a quick shower to wash away the slime and filth from the previous night's toilet war. And then, our Christmas guests began arriving. My mother would greet each new arrival with the story of our Christmas Eve encounter with the porcelain enemy and then take them into the bathroom to demonstrate how to operate the Port-A-Pot. She did this to avoid any embarrassing confusion but I believe that it was also therapeutic for her as well. And Christmas Day went off without a hitch.

Later that afternoon, after the big dinner was finished and all of the gifts opened, I stood with a glass of tea, peering through the window of our back door. There in the cold chill of a Christmas afternoon stood the white porcelain toilet that we had removed from our bathroom just 12 hours before. It was still sitting there on our back step, like a silent monument to the war that we had waged in an effort to save our Christmas traditions. We had worked so hard to clean up all of the mess and remove any obvious trace of ill activity that we completely forgot that it was still sitting out there, lid up with its white porcelain mouth open offering a cheery "Merry Christmas" to all of our guests as they arrived.

It was in that moment that I realized just how much we valued Christmas. We were literally willing to wade through sewage and foulness to save our Christmas traditions. As I turned away from the scene, I smiled to myself and chuckled, "Well, this is one Christmas that ended up in the toilet!"

A Back Porch Talkin' Christmas Carol

Growing up in the country was a special experience. Every month and season possessed events that will forever remain in my mind and close to my heart. The sights, smells, and sounds of a farm as it moved from season to season provided a magical background for a young boy who couldn't wait to grow up. Each year seemed to pass at a snail's pace, drudging from month-to-month, season-to-season, making me wonder if I would ever leave childhood behind. And then, of course, I did. I just woke up one day and discovered that I wasn't a kid anymore; the little boy was gone and was replaced by a stranger in the mirror who had to shave each day (or not). Ah, one of life's ironies; the child's desire to be an adult and the adult's desire to again be a child. But then, life itself is an irony *(thank William Shakespeare for that; not Uncle Bill)*.

Each year, when the Christmas season comes around, a melancholy wistfulness becomes intertwined with all of the happiness and cheer that I experience during this special holiday. I truly love this time of year, with all that it represents, but I must also admit that I am a bit saddened because the child in me is so far in the past that he is but a mere shadow, peering in through the window of my soul at my adult Christmas. As an adult, Christmas has a different meaning than it did as a child. Sure, there is a magic in the air, but it is a magic filled with compassion, giving, and love. But those childhood Christmases of the past were filled with a different kind of magic; a magic that represented excitement, impossibilities, and wonder.

At this point, I begin to nod off at my computer. I have been known to do that while writing; I just become so relaxed and comfortable that my head slumps forward, my eyes droop closed, and the next thing you know I am…falling…fast…aslee…zzzzzzz **[Wake up, Uncle Bill! I am the Ghost of Christmas Past.]**

Wh- What? What do you mean you're the Ghost of Christmas Past? Oh, for Pete's Sake! Now, look here! I am an English teacher and I know all about Charles Dickens and that three ghost stuff. Besides that, I am NOT a scrooge! Christmas just happens to be my favorite time of the year.

[You're not going to be visited by all three ghosts; just me. We feel you just need to go back to visit your childhood for a spell. Besides, it is a Back Porch Talkin' Christmas Story ...there is nothing more rural than a good Christmas Carol...get it? A *"Christmas Carol?"* And this is a cool way of getting Aunt Carolyn into this story...you're going Christmas Carol-in'! Hah! I just kill me! Oh wait... I'm already dead!]**

Oh, brother! A writer's fantasy ghost with a lame sense of humor! Well, you go with what works. Okay, lead on, Mac Duff! Whoops! Wrong English author. Okay, Mister Ghost...lets get this show on the road...the readers are waiting!

The room begins spinning into a foggy blur and then suddenly, I am in our old living room, looking at a beautifully decorated cedar tree with brightly wrapped presents piled everywhere under its branches. A young boy is lying on the floor, staring with wide-eyed wonder at the...

Hey! That's me! Wow! This flashback stuff is so cool! Hey, wait! I remember all of this...this is the year I got my first record player! That is when I really developed my love for music! And I also got a Major Matt Mason Moon Base and Space Port set. I was so fascinated by all of that space program stuff that was going on in the sixties...Santa Claus...well, mom and dad... bought me that space set for Christmas. I also got a set of Children's Encyclopedias that year. I read those things from cover-to-cover, you know? That was when I discovered that reading was the key to, well, to everything.

Isn't it interesting how those Christmases of the past have something to do with who I am today? Perhaps that is the real lesson in all of this; as children, we are shaped by each and every experience until one day it all carries us into our adulthood.

Within two years, I began to suspect that all of that Santa Claus stuff was fiction. I just started noticing little things about the way my parents behaved when I opened all of my gifts on Christmas morning and I have to be honest; I did snoop around a bit too much one year before Christmas and discovered some of my gifts hidden away in the attic. By the time I was ten, I knew, but I didn't let on...besides... by then my sister, Julie, was two and I didn't want to spoil all of the fun for her. So, I pretended to believe in the great bearded one until one day when my mom sat me down and spilled the beans. Gosh, I remember how difficult it was for her to tell me the truth; I didn't have the heart to tell her that I already knew the score.

[Well, Uncle Bill, it is time to get back to reality. We Christmas ghosts have to keep a tight schedule...I have to visit Larry the Cable Guy yet this evening. If you think you have problems...well, so long and I hope this little Christmas fantasy has helped. Adieu-adieu...parting is such sweet sorrow. Opps! Now I have the wrong English author! Oh, well...goodnight, Uncle Bill! Nice scaring the hell out of you this evening!]

And here I sit at my computer again. I want to thank the ghosts of my mind for allowing me the opportunity to travel back to my childhood. Despite all of this digital music that I now have, that little record player sure sounded good. And old Major Matt Mason is still the only astronaut to establish a permanent moon base and he didn't even have a cell phone! And those encyclopedias? Well, it is safe to say that they have grown into many, many other volumes in my library. Shoot, in many ways, those books played a big part in why I am writing this book at this very moment. We never really stop being children; we simply learn to separate fantasy from reality; or at least we're supposed to.

I miss the little boy that I once was; but, I suppose that innocence lost is always cherished more once it is replaced with experience. I know there are times that we all wish we could physically go back in time and change something; make a different decision or re-live a tender moment. But the hands of time just won't allow that. It is true that hindsight is twenty-twenty but innocence is blissfully blind. Christmas is a special time in our lives not only for what it represents to us as Christians, but for what it means to us as humans. It is a season of memories and experiences that carries us from childhood to adulthood and back again. It is God's time machine, a vehicle that transports us from our very beginnings to our eventual end. True, we have memories of each and every significant moment in our lives, but the memories of Christmases past are different. It is at this time of the year when the memories of our childhood help to define our adulthood. How magical is that?

So the next time the holiday season rolls around, amidst all of the fanfare and celebration, take a moment to close your eyes and drift back to a Christmas when you were a child. Re-live the magic and the wonder; breathe in the innocence and imagination; and remember who you were before time erased your youth. When you finally re-open your eyes and travel back to reality, remember that the heart of that child still beats within you, always. And that is the true miracle of Christmas.

A Moo-ving Story

So many people have packed up all of their belongings in a U-Haul and journeyed out into the countryside with the hopes and dreams of becoming *country folks*. What annoys me most about this is that once they have set up house in the country, these transplanted urbanites begin to call their little slice of heaven a *farm*. I want to set the record straight: There are a few things that every farm should have in order to be considered a farm. In fact, I believe that it is time to establish a formal code of classification for farm operations.

First and foremost, every farm should have a barn. Barns come in all shapes, sizes, and descriptions, none of which makes much difference just as long as it is a barn. If it has a roll up door, then it isn't a barn; it's a garage and a garage isn't a barn. A garage is a place where the family car is kept along with an assortment of crap that has overflowed from the house. Real farmers don't keep a boat or an RV in a barn, and you will never find Christmas decorations in there. Those things are stored in garages. If you have acreage in the country with just a garage, then all you have is acreage in the country; not a farm.

Secondly, every farm *must* have a tractor. A farm without a tractor is like an airplane without wings; it's not likely to get off of the ground. Of course, in a perfect world, every farm has a *John Deere* tractor. I can credit my late Uncle Kenneth for that brilliant piece of agricultural wisdom. Not too bad coming from an orthopedic surgeon who once purchased a John Deere tractor for his farm. Forget the fact that he never actually drove that tractor. He understood the complexity of farm classification. A farm without a tractor (John Deere or otherwise) isn't really a farm. It is just a tract of ground in the country. And for the record: a four-wheeler or a Gator is NOT a tractor; these are simply toys for overgrown boys.

Lastly but certainly not least, every farm should have at least one cow. Nothing says "I am a real farmer" like a real, live, grass-munching, pie-flopping bovine. A cow on a farm is a symbol of permanency; fences have been established, boundaries have been identified, and the owners have made a long-tem commitment. If a man (or woman) has a barn, a tractor, and a cow then they have achieved full-fledged farmership. There are in business, no matter what else takes place on that tract of land.

Of these three mandatory requirements, however, the cow is the most significant because cows add character to any farm. Why? Because cows themselves are characters. If you doubt this, then I suggest that you get to know some cows. I mean really get to know them; sit down and have some long, serious conversations with a group of cows and I believe that you agree: cows are very personable creatures. And they are great listeners, too!

My Grandpa Hornickel was in the regular habit of going out to the barn and spending time with the cows. Whenever he and my Grandma Hornickel would get into an argument, he would eventually put on his coat and hat and head out to barn where he would pull up a bale of hay and cuss at the cows for a half of an hour or so. He found this to be a much better plan of action than to actually cuss at my grandma, who, by the way, would have taken his head off with a frying pan if he would have unloaded on her. Instead, he would put some hay in the manger for the cows and while they munched, he cussed. The cows would look up every now and then and acknowledge him by nodding their heads in agreement and then go back to munching and listening. When the cows finished eating, they would moo a few low tones and then exit the barn. This was their way of saying, "Okay, we are through listening to you rant. We need to go and belch some cud and you need to go back to the house." And he would. He was satisfied, Grandma was happy, and the cows had their bellies full. What a perfect world!

Of all of the animals indigenous to the farm, the cow is cornerstone of farming heritage. From the early days of the family farm, cows were a necessary part of most farm operations because of the need for milk on demand. Without any means of mechanical refrigeration, owning a dairy cow or two was the only way for farm families to include milk, butter, and cream as a part of their dietary staple. A regular part of daily farm life included getting up before dawn and heading out to the barn to milk the cow by hand. This was done during the pre-dawn hour for two reasons: First, the cow had the nighttime hours in which to stand at rest so the mammary glands could produce and fill the lower udder with milk. Second, milk was needed for the cooking of the early day meal and for the young children in the family to drink. The side benefit to this was that whoever got the job of trudging out to the barn to do the early morning milking got to spend quality time with the cow.

As more and more people began to move away from the farms and into the big cities and towns to find work in factories and offices, the farmers discovered a new way of improving their quality of life by keeping more milk cows. Each morning, well before dawn, entire farm families would head out to the barn to do the milking. The milk was run through a hand-crank separator, strained, and placed in milk cans. These were loaded onto a wagon and hauled into a nearby city or town for bottling and distribution to urban dwellers. Each morning, fresh milk, butter, and cream was delivered to homes, restaurants, and grocery stores throughout the city or town. It was truly the beginning of farm-agribusiness; producing a needed commodity and marketing it directly to the consumer. To this very day, the dairy industry operates in a very similar fashion, though science, mechanization and refrigeration have greatly improved the quality and safety of the products.

Of course, not all cows are *dairy cows*. As refrigeration methods improved and the population of America increased, so did the need for high-yielding meat cows. Through selective breeding of several different types of bovine species, the beef cow was introduced. These cows are genetically designed to convert feed into edible muscle instead of producing high volumes of milk. On farms and ranches all across America, farmers began keeping more and more brood cows to meet the demand for beef as a food commodity. By the beginning of the twentieth century, beef had become an American dietary staple. As World War II ended, the all-beef hamburger became the mainstay of the American restaurant industry giving rise to names like McDonalds, Burger King, and Wendy's, just to name a few. By the end of the century,

74

America was annually consuming more beef than the rest of the world *combined!* And all of this began with a simple cow on the farm.

Today, beef cows are raised in every state. Calves are marketed as *feeders,* meaning that they are weaned from the cow and sold to large feedlot operations. Most commodity beef is *feedlot finished;* that is, fattened up to slaughter weight at feeding facilities that are close to the packing houses. This allows for farm producers to focus on breeding and producing calves for the beef industry. Though nearly all feedlots are large, non-farm corporate operations most of the feeder calves are still produced on family-owned farms and ranches. However, this aspect of the farming industry is now feeling the impact of the free-trade agreements of the late nineties as more and more beef is imported from South America and Asia.

Still, the cow does hold a special place in American history and heritage; after all, it was a cow that was supposedly responsible for nearly burning down the city of Chicago many years ago. Just think: Al Capone and John Dillinger couldn't bring that city to its knees but a single milk cow nearly did! Of course, some might argue that she should have moved to Washington to try her luck there. At least the loss maybe wouldn't have been as great if that town had burned down.

Cows have also been a huge part of American culture, especially in the area of marketing and advertising. Who can forget the lovable Elsie, the Cow, the spokesperson, so-to-speak, for the Borden Food Company? In the 1990s, Gateway Computers employed the most unlikely image for marketing personal computers to the world. The now most recognizable cow pattern of all: the Holstein Patches!

25 years ago, when the beef industry began to feel the pressure from the increasing popularity of poultry (now there's a mouthful, pardon the pun), they launched an advertising campaign that is still going strong today: *Beef. It's what's for dinner!* I seriously doubt that this advertising ploy would have been so successful if it had not been for the voice that they selected to deliver the message. No, the beef industry needed the voice of a

real cowboy to bring America back to the table for another helping of beef. Actor Sam Elliot's deep, cowboy drawl had consumers lining up at grocery store meat cases all across America. I personally cannot look at our cows today without hearing Sam Elliot utter, "Beef. It's what's for dinner!" Of course, Sam wasn't the first spokesperson for this marketing campaign. That honor goes to actor James Garner of *The Rockford Files* fame.

Though Europe can lay claim as the home of the modern farm cow, America is land that made the cow an icon of agricultural enterprise. Of all of the farm commodities and products raised on farms in the United States, only two are actively raised in every state, including Hawaii and Alaska: corn and cows. When you think about it, I suppose they go hand-in-hand. It takes corn to fatten beef cattle and produce milk in dairy cows. As for Al Gore worrying about all that greenhouse gas produced by cows destroying the ozone, let's worry about all those fossil fuel emissions first; then we'll address the gas that the cows pass. Besides, Al owns a cattle farm in Tennessee so he's a hypocrite anyway!

So, if you own acreage in the country, then you need to purchase a cow. You can keep it in your barn with your tractor. That way, when someone drives past your place, they'll know without a doubt that you own a farm. A garage with a four-wheeler and a goat just doesn't have the same impact. Besides, when you need someone to talk to, you'll have the perfect set of ears on hand. Goats make terrible listeners anyway. And cows usually don't charge you like a psychiatrist does. I promise you, cow ownership is truly a moo-ving experience.

Lena & Owen

The most memorable part of growing up in the country was watching and listening to the older folks. Two of my favorite rural characters were the couple who owned the farm across the county road from were I grew up. Lena and Owen, who were of the same generation as my Grandma Hornickel, were unique and colorful, each in their own right. Both possessed a very raw and often humorous way of expressing themselves verbally in nearly every situation. I was witness to this many times but one of the most memorable was a hot ,summer evening while we were trying to move two of their old sows.

Lena and Owen raised tobacco and cattle on their farm; they weren't in the business of raising hogs like we did on our farm. They did, however, keep a couple of old sows around to get a litter or two of pigs each year so they could have plenty of fresh pork to put in the freezer and a few extra to sell at market to help offset the cost. They didn't own a male hog so when they wanted to have their sows bred, they would often bring them to our farm and put them with one of our herd boars until they were bred and then take them back to their place. That was just one way that rural neighbors would help each other and this was a very natural part of farm life.

One summer, when I was about 14, in the midst of a hot, dry spell, Owen called my dad and asked if he could bring his two old sows down to have them bred. Of course, my dad said that would be okay and even offered my services of coming to get their sows with one of our big tractors and a hog transport crate. This crate was like a metal pen that mounted onto the back of the tractor and could be lowered to the ground to allow the hogs to just walk into the pen. Once loaded, the tractor lift would pick up the pen and you could drive to another location, then set the pen back down and release the hogs. It was a very handy piece of equipment.

I arrived at their farm one evening just as the sun was beginning to settle down in the western sky. Owen motioned me to a old, ram-shakled hog shed that was located out in the pasture behind the house and barns. He had already trapped the two old sows in the small, rickety shed, which had a two foot by three foot opening on one side so the hogs could go in and out. He had lured them into the shed with a bucket of feed and then covered the hole with a piece of scrap plywood. The plan was to set the transport crate down with its small slide gate up against the shed's opening, remove the piece of plywood, and then the hogs could just walk out and onto the crate. It sounded like a great plan. One problem: hogs almost never do what you want them to do.

After I placed the crate against the shed, Owen removed the piece of plywood by sliding it out to the side. We waited. Neither sow would even so much as stick their nose out of that shed and into the transport crate. So, Owen tried luring them out with some feed. Of course, the hogs were now too smart for this little trick, so Owen did just what he always did when things didn't go as planned: he began cussing at Lena, implicating her as the responsible culprit of the hogs' stubborn orneriness. His cursing wasn't just profanity; it was an eloquent mixture of the most descriptive, colorful curse words and exaggerated metaphor-filled language that anyone had ever heard. It was what I call "poetic profanity."

"Jesus H goddamned Christ! Son-of-a-bitch! What the in the hell are you doing? Don't just stand there like a goddamned dime-store Indian," he bellowed. "I'll just be goddamned!" He always had to add an exclamation to the end of every outburst. Owen glared at Lena with his one good eye; the other had been lost in an accident years before. His six foot, two inch frame was accented by his baggy old work pants, which hung low around his buttocks, threatening to fall to the ground at any moment.

Lena, who had fiery, bright red hair and stood about four feet nothing just looked at him. When he finished, she opened up on Owen with her own brand of cursing that was less colorful and a bit more raw in nature, but ever bit as much descriptive.

"Oh, shit! You old sombitch! It ain't my goddamned fault," Lena fired back. " What in the hell do you want me to do? You old bastard!"

Despite this exchange of cursing and insults, the sows still refused to exit the building. So, Owen decided that he and Lena should climb into the little shed through a window opening and chase the hogs out onto the crate. This sounded like a good idea except that Lena, because of her short stature, had trouble getting up through the window. So, Owen helped boost her up. As he did, she caught her old gingham plaid dress on an old nail and became entangled halfway in the window. More cussing and yelling ensued.

"Get the hell in there, goddamn it," Owen bellowed.

Lena fired back, "You old bastard, I'm hung on something!" A few moments of wiggling and squirming produced the loud sound of material ripping and then she finally made it through the opening, falling face-first onto the dirt and manure floor of the shed's interior. More cursing and shouting rang out from inside the old shed. Then Owen hiked his pants up so he could lift his leg high enough to reach the window and he followed.

What happened next is difficult to describe. They began trying to drive the two old sows out of the dirt floor shed. As with most old enclosed hog sheds, the floor inside was nearly a foot deep with fine, powdery dirt, kind of like a pale-tan talcum powder, made worse by the hot, dry summer. The more the hogs ran around inside and the more that Lena and Owen tried to force them out, the more the dust began to pour from every crack and opening in this old, dilapidated shed. From my vantage point on the outside, it looked as if the building was on fire with all of that fine hog shed dirt being kicked up.

"What the hell are you doing? Look out! Get out of the goddamned way! No, goddamn it, don't stand there…well, I'll be a son-of-a-bitch!"

"Well, if you would make up your damned mind, you crazy old fool. I am not a goddamned mind reader, you old bastard!"

Lena apparently had moved in front of the opening and the hogs turned back and knocked Owen off of his feet and into all of that fine dirt. The profanity spewing from the building was almost as filthy as the dust cloud that was surrounding the entire shed. One of the hogs tried to make a break for it and ran through Lena's legs, sending her down into the dust and filth. Standing outside by the hog crate, I began to snicker under my breath. As the mayhem continued, I couldn't contain myself any longer and I burst out loud with laughter. And my laughter brought an increase to the cursing and swearing from within the building. The hogs began squealing and squalling. The building began trembling and shaking, then rocking back and forth. It was total chaos. Something had to give.

And finally, it did. The rickety old hog shed began to lean, inch-by-inch, to one side, slowly falling into a nearly flat pile on the ground. As it did, both old sows found a hole and came out like rockets on fire, heading for the fenced wood lot behind the barn.

And then everything went silent. I just stood there, trying to decide what I should do. Before I could move, from inside the flattened heap came a violent chorus of cussing and profanity. Lena began to crawl through the opening where the hogs had escaped with Owen behind her trying to scramble out. In the scuffle, Lena kicked Owen right in the face with her old canvas shoe.

"Why, you old bitch! Watch out! I'll be a son-of-a-bitch! What in the hell are you a trying to do? Are you trying to goddamned kill me? Get out of the goddamned way," Owen bellowed.

When she finally made it to her feet, Lena began walking straight to the house, cussing and swearing every step of the way. Her bright red hair was almost white with dust, her glasses were coated with dirt and fresh hog manure, and her dress was torn up the back to her waist.

When Owen finally made it to his feet, he hollered to Lena, "What in Sam Hell is the matter with you?"

And then he just walked away and headed down to the barn, leaving me stand there next to the old collapsed hog shed. The heavy cloud of dust was finally beginning to settle. I stood there looking at the shambled mess, not quite knowing what I should do. Eventually, I climbed up into the tractor cab and started the engine and made the short trip home. As I pulled away, my mind began replaying the whole event and I started chuckling to myself. By the time I had parked the tractor in our barn, I was laughing so hysterically that I couldn't climb down and go into the house.

As with most every experience of growing up country, there was always something new to learn. Yes, Lena and Owen were two very special rural characters from my past and I miss them both dearly. They taught me a great deal about language and how some country folks are just defined by the way they express themselves.

Back Porch Talkin'

It's a Tractor Thing!

First, A Bit of History

In the history of agriculture, no one invention has been more significant than that of the modern farm tractor. For several hundred years, the horse was the power source that allowed farmers to grow and expand farming operations to produce more crops to keep up with the rapidly expanding population. From plowing with one-horse hand plows to pulling wagons to market, farmers began to add more horses to the hitch to increase productivity and the number of acres that could be covered in a day.

Large farm operations in the Plains States would often use massive numbers of multiple horse and mule teams numbering as high as twenty or more large draft horses to pull large tillage platforms across the rolling fields. As farming operations strained to expand, the sheer number of draft animals began to create new problems for large operations: tending and caring for all of those work animals daily. Storing enough grain and hay to maintain a large herd of draft animals was a concern for such large operations, to say nothing of the amount of time required each day to feed and groom the work animals.

Just when it seemed that agriculture had reached its growth limit, the steam engine was introduced. Beginning around 1880, the steam power age would last roughly 40 years. The pulling power of twenty horses could now be replaced with one, massive steam tractor. The added benefit was that these steam engines could also be used to power threshing machines. The only thing needed was an adequate water supply for the boiler and a fuel source. As new ground was cleared, the wood that was removed was used to fire the boilers in these massive steam engines, making them economical to operate. The downside was that they were slow and extremely heavy causing soil compaction. There were a few other drawbacks to the modern steam engine. They were usually too expensive for smaller operators to own and they required a great deal of daily maintenance to keep them operating efficiently. But then the internal combustion engine was perfected and the world of agriculture awaited the next invention that would change the face of farming forever.

In its early years, the tractor was little more than a smaller version of the steam engine with an oil-fueled hit-and-miss engine. They were awkward and cumbersome leading many early skeptics to say that the internal combustion farm tractor was just a fad; they would never replace the steam engine as stationary power source and the draft horse for field power. But early pioneers in tractor development didn't give up. They kept working to develop better engines and drive trains until the cousin of the modern farm tractor emerged and began to put the horses out to pasture. Farmers all across the country began to adapt their operations to use the tractor as their power source for everything from plowing and preparing the soil to the gathering and processing of their crops.

In 1917, the Henry Ford and Son Company created a spinoff company that began producing the Fordson farm tractor, which used some of the same drive train components of the Ford Model A. These tractors, priced at 395 dollars, were an instant hit and over 30,000 were sold by 1920.

It is significant to note that even though steam engine power was used in Europe, most of the technology and development of the modern farm tractor took place in the United States, which is of little surprise; American ingenuity has always been the driving force in industrialization and technology development. Then, in 1918, the John Deere Company made the decision to enter the world of tractor development by purchasing the Waterloo Boy Tractor Company. Though the Deere Company had been primarily involved with the development of the hardened steel plow and heavy wagon manufacturing, the company realized the real future of agriculture was in the development and refinement of a highly versatile and affordable farm tractor. The rest, as they say, is history. In 1923, after several years of development, Deere introduced the Model "D" tractor under the brand name John Deere.

Now, I am not suggesting that John Deere single-handedly revolutionized the tractor industry; in the early years of the modern farm tractor, numerous companies made significant contributions to the development of the modern farm tractor. In 1924,

International Harvester introduced the first of the Farmall line of tractors. Within six years, they were manufacturing nearly 60 percent of all farm tractors. Five years later, John Deere introduced the "GP" line of tractors with a narrow front end and wide-set rear wheels to facilitate its use in row crops. By the beginning of The Great Depression, Deere, Harvester, Case, and Allis-Chalmers stood as the dominate tractor and implement companies in the United States.

If you go to any large antique tractor show today, you'll likely see machines of every color and configuration from the early years of tractor development. Every company tried to find the magical combination of options and innovations that would become the ultimate selling point for their brand. In the end, however, it was versatility that won the great tractor war; farmers wanted tractors that could be used in every aspect of agricultural enterprise with very little on-farm adaptation needed.

In the early years, several equipment manufacturers tried marketing a tractor-plow combination. These were machines that could only be used for breaking the soil for planting. The obvious problem with this marketing strategy was that farmers were being asked to make a sizable investment on a machine that would only be used a couple of months out of the year and had no real practical application during the other seasons. This meant that the machine would be sitting in a barn somewhere gathering dust. Then, when it was needed, it took a considerable amount of tune-up work to get the engine running again. These types of tractors proved to be too impractical for wide-spread farm use.

Farmers began to look for a machine that could easily be switched from one implement to another to maximize its efficiency and initial investment cost. In addition, small-to-mid size farm operations could not justify purchasing more than one tractor; they needed a tractor that could be used for every application from preparing the soil in the spring, to making hay in the summer, to gathering crops in the fall. Some manufacturers listened to the farmers' needs while others simply went out of business.

Another selling point for most farmers was mixed brand compatibility. Most farmers wanted implements that could be used with a different brand of tractor. This meant that hitches, power sources, and remote hydraulic connections had to become universal. Companies like Deere, International Harvester, Allis Chalmers, and Oliver worked to develop industry standards for Power Take-Off (PTO) powered equipment, standard fixed-clevis hitches, and universal hydraulic power connections and controls to allow farmers to intermix different brands of tractors and implements. Again, the companies that refused to initially accept these standardizations found themselves struggling to make sales.

During World War II, Limitation Orders restricted civilian production of farm equipment and parts. All of the major tractor companies began manufacturing military equipment and war-time supplies to help the U.S. war effort and to keep remaining employees working. As part of its war effort compensation, the John Deere Company took over a steel foundry in Des Moines, Iowa and converted the plant into a heavy steel implement foundry making plows, cultivators, and forged tractor components. Over the next 25 years, agriculture expanded into a major industry and tractors become more powerful, allowing farmers to increase acreage and crop output.

However, by the beginning of the 1970's, the deciding factor for tractor manufacturers was financial stability and brand market share. Over the next fifteen years, only the strongest, healthiest companies would survive the economic downturn of agriculture and the massive inflation rates of the seventies. By 1985, only a handful of tractor companies were left and most of them had to under go mergers in order to survive. By the end of the 20th century, John Deere was the only company that had made it from the beginning of the century to the end, a 100 year span without having to merge or undergo major corporate changes in manufacturing and design. Harvester and Case had become one and Allis-Chalmers merged with the German-based Deutz machine company to become Deutz-Allis. The Massey-Harris Company had changed to the Massey-Fergusson Company while the Ford Motor Company sold off its tractor division to partner up with the Sperry-New Holland Company. Oliver was bought up by the White Heavy Engine Company and the Oliver name dropped.

Numerous foreign tractors began to make their way onto American soil like Satoh, Mahindra, and Kioti. However, these brands represented only small, estate-sized tractors and were never in contention for the large market farm tractor industry.

Many of the tractors that were manufactured fifty, sixty, or seventy yeas-ago are still running strong today, a testimony to the durability and dependability of the tractors that were being produced in the early years. At shows all across the United States, old tractors of all makes and colors stand in rows, proudly displaying their history and heritage for young and old alike. No other industrial or technological development commands as much attention or dedication as the farm tractor, truly one of the greatest agricultural developments of the Twentieth Century.

In the Beginning, God Gave Us Tractors

My dad, Ralph, started farming with his parents when he was a kid. By the time he graduated from high school, he had practically taken over the field work from his school teacher father. In 1960, he purchased an eighty acre farm for a couple thousand dollars from his grandma and grandpa and in 1961, he and my mother, Helen, were married and moved into the simple farmhouse on that farm. It had no indoor plumbing, it was heated with an old fuel oil heating stove, and it barely had electricity. In 1962, it became the place that I would call home. Most all of my childhood and adolescent memories are rooted to that tract of southern Indiana soil. Who and what I am today stems from that farm located on Hog Ridge near Laconia, Indiana.

In the early years, my dad had to rely on old, well-used machinery to prepare the ground, plant and harvest crops as he began to build and grow the farming operation. My first memory of a farm tractor was a 1950 model *50* John Deere. I don't know how old I was when I first rode on that tractor with my dad, but I do recall thinking that it was *huge!* I can vividly remember standing in front of my dad peering through that big steering wheel and hearing that distinctive *pop-pop-pop* of that old *50*'s 2-cylinder engine. From that moment, I fell in love with that tractor. Any chance I could get, I would beg to ride with dad on *my tractor!*

In 1965, my Great Uncle Clarence joined forces with my dad in the farming operation and they decided to move up to a larger tractor so they could begin to farm more ground. They purchased a new 3020 John Deere with a compliment of new, more efficient implements. I can still remember the day the John Deere dealer delivered that shiny new 3020! It was the biggest thing I had ever seen! Of course, I was just three and half years old at the time, so anything larger than the old *50* seemed *massive!*

A couple years after that, as more ground was added to the operation, dad traded the old *50* in on a lightly used 4020 Diesel, which to me was huge! Without ever realizing that it was gone, I just sort of forgot all about the old *50* Popping Johnny. *Almost…*

Time marched on and even bigger tractors were delivered to

our farm, all John Deere's, of course. As I continued to grow, so did the tractors and the number of acres that we farmed. Next, a massively big 4320 Diesel with its squared-off fenders and big, oval exhaust stack; and then, the tractor of my adolescent farm boy dreams, a Generation II 4430 with the new SoundGuard cab. I was in tractor heaven! Comfort seating; air conditioned climate; and a futuristically styled interior! What more could a country boy want? *Well...*

By the time I decided that I was grown (*my opinion, not necessarily fact*) and into adult life, the world of farming began to change. The slow down of the farm economy, the loss of a stable hog market, and bad economic times forced my dad, who was approaching mid-life, to slowly begin to taper back the farm operation. My uncle Clarence was getting up in years and it was becoming increasingly harder to make a good living from farming. We were all relying on day jobs to pay the bills and farming was becoming more of a hobby. After all, you can take the farmer out of the country; but you can't take the country out of the farmer. In terms of tractors, this meant that there would be no more new tractors coming to our farm; the ones we had would be the ones we would keep till our days were finished.

Somehow, it just didn't seem right that the tractor that had been there in the beginning wouldn't be there in the end. I began to long for that old *50* John Deere from my childhood and even though he never said so, my dad missed her too. Then, through a complex mix of circumstances that are far too complicated to explain, a *50* John Deere just like the one that dad had started farming with all those years ago made its way back into our lives and settled on our farm. It was as if the cycle was now complete; order was restored and life was as it should be. Maybe it sounds outrageous and a little exaggerated but in many ways, the arrival of that old *50* set in motion a chain of events that would forever change us all. The events and the changes are not important to this story; what is important is this old tractor is now in our lives for good.

It quickly took its place in our fleet and became "the raking tractor." Because of its size and narrow, tri-cycle front end, it is the perfect tractor for raking hay. And trust me, there is no better therapy for a middle-aged farm boy like myself than to pilot that old *50* through acres of dried hay and hear its distinctive engine sound. Operating that old tractor provides me with a connection to my heritage and my past; it is my time machine that lets me step back to a by-gone era of farming. From its seat I can feel the presence of my ancestors, smiling as they watch me continue on with the work that they began so long ago. It takes me back to my beginnings when life was simple and pure; before I had adult worries, doubts, and fears. And that's what I believe old tractors are: memory books with wheels for farm boys of any age.

Annually, for the past thirty-six years, the Lanesville Heritage Weekend in Lanesville, Indiana has offered an opportunity for people to come and walk through row after row of old tractors of every make, color, size, and configuration to revisit a place in their past that was marked by an old tractor. Just like old songs that remind you of a special moment or love in your life, old tractors take us farm folks back to a place in our past when life was simpler and the work was honest and pure. If you doubt that, just go to any antique tractor show and watch the faces of the people who slowly walk up to a particular tractor and gently, lovingly touch the hood. You can see in their eyes that they are somewhere in the past, lost in a memory that included a tractor like the one they are touching. Then slowly, they will retract their hand and walk on, eyes a bit misty, faces smiling slightly. You will have just witnessed someone taking a trip back into time and that's not science fiction, my friends; that's the power of an old tractor.

And as powerful and moving as that is to observe, those who actually own and preserve these magnificent machines experience something far deeper and even more stirring. Trust me, I know. It is not an obsession; it is a *dedication*. Rural heritage and history aside, it is about self-preservation. Taking possession of one of these old farm tractors is more about *your* past than it is about preserving the tractor. They are tangible markers of our own personal history, allowing us to share with others a place in our past that we cherish and value. They don't always mark good times or comfortable times, but they do represent a place within us that we can never truly go back to except in our hearts.

Yes, this old tractor of mine is truly a valuable piece of machinery. Not because of the work it can do or did, but because of the place in my heart that it resides: my past. This whole experience is what I refer to as *"a tractor thing."*

Hail to the Green and Yellow

When I was a youngster, I always supposed that everyone who owned a farm had tractors that looked just like ours. Everyone in our family who farmed had green and yellow tractors so it never occurred to me that there might be *(gasp)* tractors of different colors! That all changed one day when I was about six when I went with my dad to pick up some seed corn from our local Pioneer seed dealer, Henry Withers, who also farmed down in the Kintner Bottoms. Dad backed the truck up to Henry's big metal building where he housed the pallets of seed corn and there I discovered something that truly amazed me: his big tractors weren't green and yellow like ours; they were red with white trim and silver wheels. I remember walking around his big tractors cautiously like they might bite, wondering in my young mind *why* his tractors didn't look like our tractors.

Once the seed was loaded and we were headed back home (a twenty minute trip, though it seemed much longer back then. It is true; time and age are connected) I asked my dad why Henry's tractors were red instead of green. My dad laughed and said because they were a different kind of tractor, International Harvesters, my dad said. I sat quietly for a few moments and then asked my dad the 10 million dollar question: Which kind is the best?

My dad again laughed and then said, "Well, I guess that depends on what kind of tractors you have. If you have John Deere's like ours, then they are the best. If you're Henry Withers and you have Internationals, then Internationals are the best." Boy, did that shut me up! I wound up pondering that bit of philosophy for the next 42 years!

And so I grew up knowing, without a doubt, that John Deere tractors were simply the best. It was what my dad owned and my dad knew everything; what's more, my dad's cousin "Snaz" Hornickel ran the local John Deere dealership and that just confirmed this point even more. If two of the Hornickel clan had John Deere tractors, then they must be the best.

Of course, as all young boys grow, so does their curiosity about "things." I soon began to look at and notice *other* tractors. There were blue ones, and orange ones, and red ones. There were some that were two-tone orange and yellow and even some funny looking green ones with white trim. Oh, they all had similar features; a seat, a steering wheel, big tires in the back, and an exhaust stack. But somehow, they all just seemed a little odd when compared to those familiar green and yellow machines that we had on our farm. My Great Uncle Clarence even had an odd looking tractor that was short and stubby with a gray hood and fenders on a red body. My dad and great uncle always called it "the Ford" which was kind of confusing to me. After all, Ford made trucks and cars; not tractors!

Of course, by the time I reached my teens, all of this confusion cleared as I began to understand one of the great facts of life: Just as there are many different people out there in the world, so are there many different types of tractors to suit those different types of people. Once I realized that, all of this tractor diversity began to make sense. It wasn't that one brand of tractor or color was better than the other; it was that different farmers had different preferences and all of these different types of tractors each had something to offer. It was then that I began to appreciate tractors for what they really are: a reflection of individuality of their owners. Of course, for my money, John Deere's are still the best. Some things will never change!

However, I did reach a point in my life when I began to ask an all important question: Why? I could no longer just accept that John Deere's were the best just because we had always owned them. Don't get me wrong. I will bleed Deere green and yellow until the day that I die, but I did reach a point where I just wanted to know which tractor *was really* the best. I didn't have to search too hard to find the answer. In fact, answers were all around me; I just had to put all of the pieces together.

I'll start first with my late Uncle Kenneth Phillips. He spent nearly his whole adult life as an orthopedic surgeon and he made a very comfortable living, so much so that in the seventies he decided to buy a large farm near Lexington, Kentucky. He wasn't a farmer nor was he going to become one; he simply had the money and wanted a farm, so he bought one. A few months after purchasing this farm, he came home from the hospital and informed my aunt that he needed to buy a John Deere tractor. She reminded him that he wasn't a farmer and that he didn't know anything about tractors, so why did he need a John Deere tractor? His simple reply: Because every farm is supposed to have a John Deere tractor and so his farm should have one, too. Now in my mind, if a highly-educated, well-renowned Kentucky surgeon says that every farm should have a John Deere, then that is just what the doctor ordered. Score one for the John Deere's!

Growing up, there were other farmers around us that we had contact with for one reason or another. Some of these farm operations were much larger than ours and I would always get a bit jealous when ever we would visit them, in part because they usually had more tractors than did we. And most of these big operations had John Deere tractors and machinery. It just stands to reason that if the big boys are using Deere, then it must be the best stuff. You don't become super successful in the farming industry by using sub-standard equipment. To be number one, you have to go first-rate all the way. Take Hauswald Farms, for example. They have so many John Deere tractors; they can't even remember where all of them are. Plus they have a big farm shop with John Deere bar stools at the workbench, a John Deere clock, and even John Deere coffee cups to enjoy their coffee in. Only the best tractor company would have all of that stuff. Get my drift? Score another point for The Green Team.

The final selling point for John Deere's reputation as the best is that John Deere became the first tractor company to become a cult symbol in America. Actor Ashton Kutcher and Johnny Knoxville were showing up on TV and in movies wearing their John Deere caps and President George W. Bush was always tooling around his Texas ranch on his John Deere Gator. Hell, even Kevin Bacon was driving a 2940 John Deere in his break-through movie, *Footloose*. The way I figure it, if John Deere is good enough for the Hollywood stars and presidents of the United States, then it has to be the best machinery line in America. All across the country, owning something, *anything* that sports the name John Deere on it has become an elite status symbol, like driving a BMW or wearing a Rolex watch. Slam dunk! Game over. John Deere wins, hands down!

Now I realize there will be some who read this who will say, "Uncle Bill, you're dead wrong! This brand or that brand is the best." And all I can say to that is that everyone is entitled to their opinion, even if they *are* in denial. I don't need any further convincing: John Deere tractors are the best tractors ever made. Period. All the rest can fight over second place. Of course, there is truth in the statement that *all tractors* are special because they represent someone truly great in our heritage and history: the American Farmer. When you think about tractors in that context, color and make doesn't really matter. I could have also said that size doesn't matter but that would just make some of you guys uncomfortable, so I'll leave that topic for another digression. What is significant is that farm tractors have played a key role in making American agriculture superior to the rest of the world. Besides, it is the best way that I know to end this argument without giving in.

Nothing Says Love Like a John Deere

One of my favorite memories from "the good old days" was when our local John Deere dealer, which just happened to be my dad's first cousin, Lorrel "Snaz" Hornickel, would host the annual "John Deere Day" each winter. It was always held on a Saturday when all of the local farmers were chomping at the bit to get past winter and head into the fields to begin the spring planting season. Besides, most farmers had all of their crops off to market by then making it a great time to entice them to purchase a new piece of machinery. Everyone would arrive around 10:00 a.m. and grab a complimentary bag lunch consisting of a ham sandwich, a bag of potato chips and a doughnut. They would have a bunch of bottled soft drinks iced down in a couple old wash tubs and one of the guys from the shop would be standing there with a towel and a bottle opener to wipe your bottle down and pop your cap. Then, everyone would find a place to sit and eat this country boy's gourmet meal in brown paper and discuss everything from farming to basketball. Actually, this could also be referred to as gossipin' but everyone knows that real men don't gossip; they *discuss*.

The real highlight of the event, however, was after the meal when they would herd everyone out into the shop which had been transformed into an impromptu movie theater by adding some folding chairs borrowed from a local church and erecting a huge movie screen at one end. A corporate executive from the John Deere Company would get up, tell a few lame jokes, and say a few words about the new products for the upcoming year. Then, someone would kill the shop lights and the movie would start. Each year, The John Deere Company would spend a considerable sum of money putting together a film to show at John Deere Day events all over the United States. These films were usually a blend of new products and farm technology, history and heritage, and humor. For a farm boy like me, it was a great way to spend a Saturday with my dad. In fact, most John Deere Day crowds were made up of fathers and sons; it was pretty much an all-guy event. There were, however, a few ladies in the crowd each year and by the time I was in my teens, this became a point of fascination for me: Could there really be females in this world who actually *enjoy* looking at tractors and farm machinery?

Now, I knew that women had to sometimes operate tractors; my mom and Aunt Betty both had plenty of experience pulling a hay wagon around the field while the men-folk pitched hay up to my dad, who was always the designated stacker. But that is where their interest in tractors ended. No, I am referring to women who would actually rather spend time looking at farm machinery than handbags at an outlet mall. Perhaps this *tractor thing* wasn't an all-male sport after all.

When I was 17, I attended the Future Farmers of America national convention in Kansas City, Missouri. While sitting there in that huge convention center with 25,000 other FFA members, I met a girl from Nebraska. We hit it off and spent several hours talking about farming, FFA, and how much we loved living in the country. I mentioned that I especially loved harvest time because I liked hauling corn from the field in the big gravity wagons and dumping the corn into the elevator and watching it go up into the grain bin. Her eyes got big and she excitedly proclaimed that she loved doing that, too! I was stunned.

I looked at her and asked, "You actually haul the corn with a big tractor and wagons?"

She looked at me with a slight smirk and said, "Well, yeah! We have a 1000 bushel auger cart and an 8640 John Deere. I bring the corn to our grain center and dump it in the holding tank so it can go up in the grain leg to one of our batch dryers."

I shifted uneasily in my seat. I nervously looked around to see if anyone around us had been listening. Holy Cow! This babe has a *bigger* tractor than I do! Talk about feeling self-conscious! Then, as nonchalantly as possible, I asked, "How many acres does your dad farm?"

"*We* farm *6000* acres," she replied abruptly. "There's my mom and dad, my three sisters, and me. My mom, dad, and older sister run the combines and my other two sisters and I haul the corn." I sat there looking at her in disbelief: I was actually conversing with an attractive, tractor-driving goddess from the Great Corn Belt. I must have been dreaming! And then she told me that she wished that I lived in Nebraska so I could take her to the prom that coming spring. "All of the guys that I go to school with call me a freak cause I drive a tractor and do farm work," she said.

And that was when I discovered that apparently all of the teenage guys in Nebraska were dumbasses. They actually believed that this attractive, brown-eyed, blonde-haired, well-built, tractor-driving, corn-farming, sweetheart was a freak? What craziness! When I got home from Kansas City, my parents asked me if I had leaned anything at the convention. I told them that I discovered that I wanted to move to Nebraska. I didn't, of course. *Damn it!*

Now that I am older and wiser *(again, my opinion; not necessarily fact)*, I have since learned that there are actually a few females out there who genuinely do love tractors. I know that this may be hard for some of you to believe, but I know that there are some women who would rather receive a beautifully restored *60 John Deere* for Valentines Day than a box of cheap chocolates and a dozen roses. Yes, I know that these tractor-loving goddesses are rare, but make no mistake about it; they do exist! The real mistake that most single country boys make is that they look for these gals in all of the wrong places. You're probably not going to find a real tractor mama at a disco dance club or on a tropical cruise to the Bahamas. And I doubt that you'll find many tractor babes at a single's bar unless of course that particular single's bar is located in the middle of a corn field in rural Illinois and is called The Hay Loft Inn.

I know of one guy who actually met his wife at the National Farm Machinery Show in Louisville, Kentucky. He was standing there looking at a tractor display when he noticed these two ladies walking around the tractor with a misty gleam in their eyes. Nervously, he moved over next to them and casually asked if they had ever seen anything as beautiful as that big, shiny tractor. When the brunette made the statement that "this new tractor was sure pretty, but she still loved her old 4020," this fellow knew he was in love. After all, it isn't everyday that you find a single, attractive woman who not only knows what a 4020 *is* but actually owns one.

Ah, love. Theirs was courtship that consisted of tractor shows and moonlit drives on a big, old John Deere. They were married a year later. The bride insisted that her bride's maids all wear sun-yellow gowns with John Deere Green sashes. The groom even wore a John Deere cap down during the ceremony. Most of the men in attendance wept openly. It was a beautiful moment.

And speaking of beautiful moments, a few years back, I was witness to one of the most moving wedding moments that I had ever experienced. One of our neighbor boys, Chad Schweitzer, and his bride, Cara, held their wedding in the middle of a big field on his parent's farm, just up the road from our place. With everyone attired in jeans and sitting on bales of hay, the groom arrived on the scene driving a beautifully restored Allis-Chalmers pulling a wagon with all of the groomsmen on-board while the dee-jay played *She Thinks My Tractor's Sexy*. I could feel the lump grow in my throat and mist begin to creep into my eyes.

Then, some fellow that I know leaned over to me and said, "Isn't that great? It was all Cara's idea!" And that did it for me. My tears flowed like a river. I quickly pulled a hanky from my pocket and as I was wiping my eyes and blowing my nose, I noticed my long-time farmer friend, Doug Keys, sitting across the hay bale aisle, pulling his blue bandana from his hip pocket to mop the stream from his eyes as well. A tractor in the wedding ceremony; how much more beautiful could it get?

Of course, not all tractor mamas started out as tractor mamas; some of them grew up playing with Barbie dolls, wearing makeup, and doing all those other typical "girl" things. But then one day it happened; they saw their first shiny red International 1066 and their world was changed. They began to dream of the day when they would ride off into the sunset on a big, shiny, powerful tractor. If they happened to find a man who already had a 1066, then all the better; just as long as he let *her* drive the tractor and not just ride on it. In fact, a real tractor mama dreams of finding a husband who is willing to *give* her the 1066 as a wedding gift. After all, her interest is in the tractor; not the man. He is just a convenient bonus in the whole scheme of things.

For me personally, I had all but given up finding a woman who could appreciate the beauty and grace of a well-built farm tractor. And then I met Carolyn. At first, I didn't have much hope; after all, Carolyn grew up in the city. But when she mentioned to me that she did her own mechanic work and was a real whiz at rebuilding a carburetor, I felt a swooning in my chest. She told me that she used to spend her summers and weekends at her grandparents farm, but they didn't really have any tractors to speak of. I knew that there was one sure-fire way to find out if there was a real tractor mama hiding beneath that beautiful exterior, so I took her to the National Farm Machinery Show. And right there before my very eyes, I watched with absolute amazement as she transformed from a mild-mannered urban girl into a tractor loving woman! It was an amorous moment when her gaze fell upon that new John Deere 6420. Her eyes softened as she climbed up into the cab of that fabulous machine and stared out over its hood. Her hands gently gripped the wheel as she gingerly touched the controls. I looked up into the cab and asked, "Well, what do you think?"

She looked down at me with eyes that made me shudder and replied in a low, sexy voice: "I want one!" I looked to the heavens and silently mouthed, *"Thank you, God!"*

Now, whenever hay season comes around, Carolyn is always ready to rake hay with *"her"* old 50 John Deere. And I have to tell you, for an old farm boy like me, there is no greater turn-on than to see my wife perched up on that green and yellow machine, chugging along with a 5-bar wheel rake in-tow, rolling that aromatic, sundried hay out into long, graceful windrows under a bright blue, Indiana summer sky. Just writing about it makes me all warm and fuzzy inside. *Seriously.*

Maybe it's no accident that the National Farm Machinery Show is always held in mid-February each year. Yes, I know that they "say" it is because it is the best time for farmers to get away for a day, but I believe there is a much deeper reason. Nothing says "I Love You" more than strolling hand-in-hand down the rows of beautifully sculpted and masterfully crafted farm tractors.

I'll close with a dual message: First, for all of you tractor loving guys out there: Women and tractors are a lot alike; they both need care and attention if you hope to keep them around for a long time.

Just remember: Love your wife and like your tractor. Take her for a nice tractor ride to a remote location and then FORGET THE TRACTOR for a while! She'll love you for it!

And for you ladies, I offer this: Men never grow up. They are always going to be little boys and little boys do like their toys. If you ever get the feeling that your man loves his tractor more than he loves you, then try this: Slip into something really sexy, climb up on his tractor, and sincerely ask him to take you for a ride. My bet is that you'll discover that he'd rather play "house" than play with his tractor. Besides, every little tractor boy *loves* his tractor mama! Think about it!

If You Ain't Broke, Then Fix It!

Eugene Gleitz once told me there are only two kinds of tractors: the kind that run and the kind that don't. Of course, all tractors were brand new at one time and they would start on the first turn of the crank. This is when the owner was the happiest; when he or she (yes, there are a few female tractor owners) could just climb up on their machine, fire it up, and go to work. But with time, tractors, like some people, begin to get cantankerous and develop attitudes especially when the comes time to get something done. From personal experience, nothing can turn an afternoon of cutting hay into drudgery faster than a tractor that is suffering from a bad case of the breakdowns. There's one thing I can tell you for certain: cursing and calling the tractor every nasty name in the book won't make it run any better nor will it improve the mood of the owner. It is kind of like trying to teach a pig to sing: It wastes your time and it annoys the pig.

Now, some tractor owners are first-rate mechanics who can fix just about any problem in short order and be back at work in no time at all. Our neighbor, Tom Branham, is one of those rare mechanic gurus who just have the in-born knack for fixing things when they break. I used to say that Tom could rebuild a tractor engine with some spare parts from a '57 Chevy, an old set of cultivators, and two discarded Maytag washing machines. The amount of mechanical knowledge that he has in his head could fill a library and I am glad that I got to spend some quality shop-time with him because I learned some valuable things. After all, he taught me how to clean and gap a set of points with an old matchbook. Of course, I never have an old matchbook when I need to clean and gap a set of points so I just had to adapt that process to using a nail file and a piece of heavy paper.

Not all tractor owners, however, are as mechanically adept as Tom. In fact, some are just down right ignorant when it comes to keeping their tractors running. I have known several guys who lived by the philosophy that tractors are built to last forever and when they do finally quit running, then it is just time to buy a new tractor. The funny thing about these guys is that they don't trade in the broken tractor; instead, they just pull them off somewhere to abandon them in the weeds. I suspect that they don't trade in the tractor because they don't want anyone to discover that they can't fix the darn thing. If you happen to spy that broken tractor and offer to buy it from them, they usually just say something like, "No, I wouldn't feel right about selling you that piece of old junk." Again, the probable reason is that they don't want you to discover that they couldn't fix a minor problem, so they would rather just let the tractor rust away. And so it just sits there until it is a rusted-up hulk of iron. Then, once it is good and rusted over, they end up giving it to some sap who convinces them that they are doing them a favor by getting that hunk of junk out of their way. In days past, Tom Branham would usually be that sap and he'd drag that old tractor home. Two hours later, with the help of a book of matches and a can of WD-40, he'd have that old rusted hunk of tractor running like a top.

Buying an old tractor to fix up can be a very expensive venture, especially if you want to restore it to "new" condition. Depending on the make, model, and condition, a total tractor restoration can run into the tens of thousands of dollars. For example, if you decide to locate a late 60's model John Deere 4020 Diesel as a project tractor, keep in mind that new tires all the way around can run at least 2500 dollars and that is if the rims are in perfect shape with little or no rust out. If the engine needs a total overhaul including injectors and pump, add another 4000 to your budget. And if you have to split the tractor in half, then you'll probably want to rebuild the clutch while you're at it. Add another 1000 dollars. Of course, you'll want to replace any and all broken fixtures and accessories including the seat, the steering wheel, rusted-out fenders, and damaged side-screens which can easily run you over a couple thousand dollars. 4020 John Deere's have extensive hydraulic systems which can be very costly to rebuild, depending on how many hours the tractor has on it to begin with. When you consider that the average cost of a 4020 project tractor is around 9000 dollars, you can have over 25,000 tied up in a total rebuild! Of course, when you're finished, you will have a very dependable and versatile tractor that can be used for just about any small-to-mid size farm and estate job. And in my opinion, a John Deere 4020 that has been carefully and meticulously restored is one of the most beautiful tractors around. But again, I *am* biased. Mr. Spock and I both have green blood, I guess.

Of course, not all old tractor enthusiasts are into restoring the tractor to "new" condition. For many, just getting an old relic to run like a top is more than enough to satisfy their lust for ageless iron. The fenders could be falling off of a completely rusted WC Allis Chalmers, but if it purrs like a kitten, then that is all that is required for some folks. Country humorist and writer, Roger Welsch, began restoring old Allis Chalmers after he "inherited" an old WC. His general theory is that fresh paint and new decals just hides the nostalgia of the machine underneath. He prefers to restore the tractor to new running condition while leaving the exterior untouched, exploiting instead the function of the machine as opposed to form and appearance.

There are other benefits to undertaking a tractor restoration. Depending on the individual, working for several hours each evening in the shop can be very therapeutic. The sheer act of disassembling an intricate machine and then meticulously putting it back together to better-than-new condition can be a very rewarding and satisfying experience. Personally, I find that escaping from the daily pressures of life to immerse myself in a good tractor mystery is a great way to good mental health.

For others, the act of restoring a tractor can lead to high blood pressure, sleeplessness, and premature hair loss. Worse case, it can lead to bankruptcy, varicose veins, and divorce. The important thing to remember when deciding to begin a restoration project is that tractors, like fine wine, bacon, and women are best when enjoyed in moderation. Oh, I know some of you guys out there will argue that last point, but reality is when you drink a soda every time you are thirsty, pretty soon you'll lose your taste for the soda and it won't quench your thirst anymore. If any of you figure out what I am talking about, then write or call me and let me know. All I'm saying is just don't let a tractor restoration become an obsession.

Just remember, tractor ownership should never be taken lightly;

it requires a commitment that nearly equals that of marriage. Before you jump in and say "I do," remember that you are making a promise to love, honor, and obey, in sickness and in health, until death do you part. There is also a line in there about forsaking all others which, by the way, means to keep your eyes, hands, and any other wandering part of your anatomy away from any other stray tractor that comes rolling down the lane with its engine revved up and its seat all soft and supple.

And just as a friendly piece of advice, you might want to adhere to these same rules when it comes to your marriage and your chosen darling person. Funny thing about spouses; they generally expect you to live by those marriage vows. If not, you're liable to find yourself out in the cold without a spouse, a home, or a tractor! Which reminds me, before you say "I do" you might want to get a prenuptial agreement signed that excludes your tractor from any property division in the event that you can't uphold your end of those previously mentioned wedding vows. Losing a wife to divorce is a rough situation. Losing your tractor in the divorce to your wife is pain beyond comprehension.

There is, however, another approach to tractor restoration but I want to warn you up front: you're gonna need deep pockets! If you are one of those guys who can't tell a pair of Vice-Grips from a pair of Channel-Locks, then you may want to consider hiring a professional tractor restorer to do the job. There are some guys out there who have turned their knack for tractor mechanics into a business. It is kind of like *Pimp My Ride* goes country. I should warn you, however; always get some references. Go and look at their work before you commit a year's salary on the whole project. Just because someone *says* they restore tractors doesn't mean that they are any good at it. I suppose that is true of so many things in life. I have met people who claim they can sing like a bird and when they favor you with a tune, it turns out that they meant a buzzard dying of heat stroke in the middle of the highway! Again, hiring someone else to restore your old tractor will generally not be cheap. Get an estimate up-front and get it in writing! If the person can't write, you might want to pass on their services; after all, incompetence begins with ignorance. Damn! That sounds so philosophical!

On the other hand, if you have the extra time and an adequate place to work, undertaking a tractor restoration job can be an excellent way to expand your knowledge of mechanics. If you don't own a good set of mechanics tools, Cresent offers a really nice set of high quality mechanics tools for around 150 dollars. This should be sufficient to get you started. Of course, there is always Walmart; most offer a nice selection of Stanley mechanics tools that are priced modestly. Then, you can add a few specialty tools along the way without draining your budget. Of course, you'll want to pick up an I & T shop manual for your specific make and model tractor, which can be obtained at most farm supply centers for around 25 bucks. My last piece of advice is to locate a few guys who have expertise in the area of ag mechanics. Most are more than willing to share some of their vast tractor mechanical know-how with you, though I do want to forewarn you: you may have to listen to several tall-tales before they will impart their tractor wisdom on you. In the game of tractor restoration, story-telling and tall-tales are the norm. Just be prepared to listen.

As you can see, classic tractor ownership can be a serious commitment. But it can also be enjoyable, too. Once you have restored your old classic, you may want to consider attending a few antique tractor shows and displaying your piece of agricultural history. You can meet some really nice folks and spend some time sharing stories and knowledge with other tractor enthusiasts. It will give you a warm and fuzzy feeling inside when someone stops to admire your tractor and ask you all about it. Just make sure that you have a couple of good tall tales to tell while you are imparting your knowledge to them. You'll make Eugene Gleitz so proud if you do. Until next time, keep your throttle wide open and your backside in the seat.

Hollywood Tractors

When the first farm tractors made their way from the drawing boards and minds of those innovative engineers to the farms and ranches all across this great country, the tractor manufacturers never dreamed that this great American invention would one day evolve into the icon of farming around the world. Today, in even the most urban of settings, when someone mentions farming, the first image that comes to mind is a farmer on his tractor. It is what non-farming America can witness from the Interstates and highways that traverse the nation and has become the most visible representative of the agricultural industry today. Most American children can't tell you where milk comes from but when asked what a farmer drives, they are quick to answer, "A tractor!"

Oh, we have songs about tractors, though most are "country" songs. That is if you consider modern "country music" to be "country music." *She Thinks My Tractor's Sexy,* for example, makes the point that some women are apparently suckers for sun burned, overall wearing, tractor driving farm boys. On the other side of that argument, I have yet to see scantily-clad tractor groupies lining up around our fields, with tongues wagging and eyes popping, in hopes of catching the attention of some tractor operator *(like me!)*; however, it is a nice thought.

Over the years, Hollywood has been reluctant to include the tractor in their films. It is my guess that most of those Hollywood directors realized that they didn't know diddly-squat about tractors so they just opted to leave them out of the picture, so to speak. One of my best examples is in the Kevin Costner film, *Field of Dreams,* where a 60's hippy-turned-Iowa-corn-farmer begins hearing voices in his corn field. *"If you build it, he will come,"* the voice whispers. This prompts the main character to plow up his nearly tasseled corn to build a baseball field for a bunch of dead baseball greats to play on. Costner's character is then shown on his John Deere tractor pulling some type of brush mower through the corn. The problem is, the PTO shaft is in full view in the scene and it is clearly *not turning!* Yes, that is a minute detail, I suppose, but we are talking about realism here. After all, Hollywood is responsible for all of those films that turn fantasy into reality. You'd have thought that having the PTO shaft turning would have been an important visual effect.

Even the old TV favorite, *Green Acres,* had problems when it came to filming Oliver Wendell Douglass (Eddie Albert) driving his rusty old tractor into a scene. It seems that Mr. Albert couldn't master the art of operating the hand clutch on the old classic John Deere GP. I realize that acting takes a great deal of brain power, but it is baffling how one cannot grasp the simple concept of pushing a lever forward to go and then pulling that same lever back to stop. I guess what disturbs me most is that Mr. Albert was a real-life war hero before he was an actor. In World War II, during the D-Day invasion, Eddie Albert commanded a squad of men at Omaha Beach and was awarded an accommodation for his actions. For that, I do applaud him. However, it just doesn't make any sense how a man who could face down a hail of German machine gun fire and keep his cool under the pressure of battle couldn't manage to operate an old, rusty John Deere tractor for 20 seconds on a TV show? To film the scene, a chain was tied to the front of the tractor and it was pulled by an old Ford van owned by the studio. All Mr. Albert had to do was ride on the tractor for about twenty feet while it was pulled by the van and then reach out and pull back on a lever. The tractor was not even running in the scene; the sound was over-dubbed in post-production. I know that *Green Acres* was a comedy farce, but how lame!

Hey, if anyone out there really believes that Kevin Bacon was actually driving that tractor in that game of tractor chicken in the 80's dance film classic, *Foot Loose,* please contact me; I have some prime swampland in Arizona that I want to sell you. Mr. Bacon, himself, let that cat out of the bag.

"There was no way that I was going to actually drive that tractor! Most of the close-ups of me on that machine were shot up-close with a wind machine blowing my hair. I had a stunt double that did the actual driving sequences."

And that just baffled me when I discovered that somewhere in Hollywood there is a tractor driving stunt-double for Kevin Bacon. Seriously, how much demand is there for a stunt man who resembles Kevin Bacon *and* can operate a tractor?

In my search for more information on tractors that have graced the silver screen, I came across a blog site entitled, *Tractors in Movies.* For those of you who don't know, a blog site is a kind of "liar's bench" on the World Wide Web. I read through nine pages of blog posts and the hands-down winner for a tractor in a movie was from *Days of Thunder* staring Tom Cruise and Robert Duvall. In one scene, Mr. Duvall, who plays a NASCAR crew chief by the name of Harry Haugg (only in Hollywood!) is out on his International 1066 spraying something on a field of young soybeans when he is visited by local car dealer, Tim, played by actor Randy Quaid. As Quaid walked along on the ground in front of the tractor, Mr. Duvall is shown actually driving the big International that is pulling a functioning sprayer. At one point, Duvall stopped the tractor and shut down the engine to have a brief conversation with Quaid before restarting the machine and continuing on down the field.

Investigating further into this Hollywood tractor moment, I discovered that Mr. Duvall was actually operating the tractor in the scene. He was asked by the director if he knew how to drive a tractor and he replied, "Yes, I own several on my ranch. I can drive them better than I can a car."

I knew there was a reason why Robert Duvall is one of my favorite Hollywood stars. And so, the Oscar for Tractor Driving in a Major Motion picture goes to... Robert Duvall and his International 1066 in the NASCAR thriller, *Days of Thunder!*

I guess the real question in my mind is why Hollywood hasn't produced a motion picture that features the tractor in a more central role? Cars have dominated films and TV for years as "non-human characters." Michael J. Fox went *Back to the Future* in a Delorean time machine. Burt Reynolds turned the black 1977 Firebird Trans Am into "The Bandit." And don't forget those damned Duke Boys and their creek-jumping Dodge Charger, "The General Lee."

Oh, we have watched movies with trucks, both big and small; all kinds of films featuring aircraft of every size and description; and there have been more films made highlighting the adventures of watercraft from log rafts to nuclear attack submarines. Let's not forget to mention all of those astronauts and their spaceships: Jim Lovell and Apollo 13; Hans Solo and the Millennium Falcon; and Captain James T. Kirk and the Starship Enterprise...times two. And still no feature films staring a hero and his trusty John Deere. What the hell is wrong with Hollywood? Well, I could go into that but it would take another entire book just to sort out that town. Let's just say that it is a good thing that Hollywood and Washington, D.C. are on opposite ends of the country!

Just think: a major motion picture featuring Tom Hanks as a Midwest dairy farmer. Why Tom Hanks? Well, he has successfully perfected every other type of character on the silver screen, so why not a Midwest dairy farmer? When he becomes so enraged over the lack of a government price support for milk, he sets out on his 4430 John Deere to take his message to the people in every state, becoming a cult hero in the process. As he travels, he is joined by more and more disgruntled farmers until he finally makes his way to Washington, D.C. with thousands of farmers from all across the country following on tractors of every size, make, and description. Just as congress is preparing to vote down an important farm bill that would save dairy farms across the country, the huge parade of tractors descends on the nation's capital, grid-locking the city and creating a media frenzy that forces the congress to reconsider and do the right thing. That in its self is pure fiction. Just imagine...Congress doing the right thing!

At the end of the film, Hanks would climb up in his trusty 4430 and head for home a national hero. And at the center of all of this is would be the tractor, the tangible icon of American agriculture. Well, I think it could make a great movie. Of course, I *am* biased!

Seriously, when is Hollywood going to make a film that focuses on the life and times of John Deere? From the forged steel plow to the largest farm equipment manufacturer in the world...what a story! Or how about how Henry Ford revolutionized the farming industry with the release of the Fordson tractor? Any film about Ford family is bound to be dramatic. With all of the movies that Hollywood has produced focusing on the world of auto racing, why couldn't they make just one that exploits the drama and excitement of Championship Tractor Pulling? I can just see the movie trailer now for the new, action-packed, tractor-pulling, drama-thriller featuring an all-star cast: George Clooney, Billy Bob Thornton, Dennis Quaid, Julia Roberts, Jennifer Aniston, John C. Reilly and Tim McGraw. I even have the perfect title: Coming to a theater near you... *Full Pull!* Hell, maybe *I* should write for Hollywood!

Home for Christmas

There is nothing quite as nostalgic as a white Christmas in the country. Around this part of the country, it is rare to have a descent snow fall on Christmas; our first snow usually comes a few weeks later in January. But on those rare occasions when we have been lucky enough to get a good snow on Christmas Eve, those of us who live out here in the country have the opportunity to experience a true storybook Christmas. The last respectable snowfall at Christmas was in 2004 when we ended up with 16 inches on the ground here on Hog Ridge. It was a white Christmas to remember, that's for certain! Of course, in today's world of holiday travel, a good snow on Christmas can cause some problems for families who must journey across distances to spend time with their kin at this special time of the year. Back in the days before the modern interstates and paved highways, winter travel could be almost impossible.

This story is about how one old tractor and its owner helped save Christmas for a family during World War II.

For most rural families, the war was a difficult time; many young farm boys found themselves half way around the world in places and situations that they could have only imagined in their worst nightmares. For the loved ones they left behind, day-to-day life was often a struggle. The farm economy, still reeling from the Great Depression, was trying desperately to survive amid the conflict of world war and many farmers all across the country were forced to find work in war plants to help pay the bills and keep the family farm going.

John was a third generation farmer who lived in rural southern Indiana. In 1943, two of his sons, Nathan and Andrew, were in the Navy fighting the Japanese somewhere in the South Pacific. With farm prices bottoming out and very little money coming in, John was forced to find work at a war plant in Evansville to help pay the bills. While he lived in a boarding house and worked a 12 hour-shift each day, his wife, Clara, and the two younger children, Susan, 16, and Thomas, 12, managed the family dairy farm. Traveling home from Evansville on weekends was challenging when the weather was good; any sizable amount of snow and the trip would be nearly impossible. As Christmas approached, John was determined as ever to make it home to spend time with his family. On the morning of December 24th, just as John climbed aboard the old bus that would carry him home, a blinding, heavy snow began to fall. With no modern snowplows or salt trucks to keep the road clear, travel soon became difficult. By nightfall, the bus finally made it into Jasper. A policeman stepped up onto the bus and told the few remaining passengers that the snow was just too bad and the roads to the east were all impassable; the bus would not be traveling any further that night.

John grabbed the bag of gifts that he had with him, pulled his collar up around his neck, and set out on foot toward his farm in Orange County, still some 20 miles away. It was dark and cold with blinding snow blowing at his back as he moved through the nearly foot-deep snow on the road. By 9:30, John was 10 miles from his farm, but he realized that he was completely numb from the cold. He was fighting the urge to lay down in the snow and go to sleep because he was so tired from walking. In the pit of his stomach, John realized that he wouldn't make it home to celebrate Christmas with his family. He also knew that he had to find shelter and warmth soon or he would surely die. In the distance, he saw the faint glow of a farmhouse with smoke coming from the chimney. He would have to stop and hope that whoever lived there would take mercy on him and allow him to warm himself and rest.

When he reached the front door of the big, white farmhouse, his body was so cold he had trouble knocking on the door. When the finally door opened, an older man in overalls and wire frame glasses eyed him up and down and asked him in. As the old farmer helped John to a chair by the wood stove, his wife put on a pot of coffee and brought out a big plate of homemade cookies. Within few minutes, John was finally able to speak and told the couple why he was out walking in a winter storm on Christmas Eve.

"I can't believe that I am not going to make it," said John to the older fellow. "A man should be with his family on Christmas, especially now. I am less than 10 miles from home. I have just got to get there." The old farmer looked at John and then asked, "You have any sons in the war?" "Two, both Navy" John replied. "My boy was a pilot," the old man said quietly. When he didn't continue, John looked across the room to a piano against one wall. On it was a framed photo of a handsome, young aviator. Then John saw the neatly folded American flag lying next to the photo and he knew. "I'm sorry,' he said. "How long ago," he asked softly. "This past September…he was twenty-four. His bomber went down somewhere over Germany. He was our only son." For a moment, everything was quiet as John stared at the floor. He wanted to say more, but couldn't find the words. Sometimes, there just are no words to say. Then the host stood up abruptly and said, "You know, you're right about one thing…a man should be with his family on Christmas. Come on, son…let's get you home!"

John slowly stood and said, "Thanks, but the roads are completely covered. I don't think you should take a truck out on a night like this." The old farmer turned with a twinkle in his eye and said, "We ain't takin' a truck. We're takin' a John Deere!"

They headed out to the barn were the old farmer keep his "D" John Deere. Within a few minutes, he had the tractor fired up and running. They hooked a two-wheeled cart up to the tractor, put in a couple extra cans of fuel, just in case, and then John climbed in with his bag and a thermos of coffee, courtesy of the farmer's wife. They headed out the farm lane and onto the snow covered road. The steel-cleated wheels on the old "D" had no problem with the snow covered roads. John leaned back and watched as the old man steered the tractor through the snow and darkness for over an hour until he finally saw the crossroad that led to his farm. He yelled out, motioning to the left and the old farmer responded. Twenty minutes later, they pulled up into the yard in front of John's house. Clara came out onto the front porch followed by their two younger children. They stood in amazement as John jumped down out of the cart and walked up the steps. He hugged his wife and children. Clara cried, of course; women always do.

Then, to John's amazement, two more figures walked out the front door and stood on the porch, both wearing white Navy uniforms. His sons had made it home for Christmas; a true Christmas miracle! The old farmer, surveying the scene, smiled as a tear escaped from one eye and rolled down his cheek in the icy, night air.

After a few more moments of tear-filled reunion with his now complete family, John walked back to the old man on the still running John Deere. He stuck out his hand and said, "How can I ever thank you enough? What do I owe you?" The old man grasped John's hand and smiled, "Son, you don't owe me anything. Merry Christmas and may God Bless all of us." And with that, the old farmer engaged the hand clutch and steered the tractor and cart out of yard and onto the lane. Within a few moments, he had disappeared into the cold, snowy night. John watched until the sound of the tractor was replaced by the silence of the falling snow; then he and his family headed into the house to continue their reunion.

The next morning, as John sat in his chair gazing at the Christmas tree, his mind couldn't forget the kindness of the farmer and his wife and it saddened him to think that the kind old couple was spending this Christmas alone with only the memory of their son. Suddenly, John leapt to his feet and shared an idea with his family, who all immediately sprang into action. Roughly an hour later, the whole family was piled onto a wagon, snuggled up under blankets as John drove his International tractor along the same snowy road he had just traveled a few hours before. Within an hour, they were pulling up into the yard of the old farmer, bringing with them their complete Christmas dinner and a few hastily wrapped gifts. For the next several hours, they laughed and shared the fellowship of Christmas with the old couple who had unselfishly opened their home and hearts on a cold, snowy Christmas Eve.

Of course, the war eventually ended and both of John's sons returned home to the family farm, where they worked with their dad to expand their dairy operation. They remained close friends with the older farmer and his wife, spending holidays throughout the year in each other's company. In 1954 the older farmer died suddenly of a heart attack. His wife was forced to sell their farm and was thankful when John's oldest son, Nathan, became the new owner. The John Deere "D" that had carried John home on that snowy Christmas Eve was now a part of their family.

In 1998, John passed away. His four children, nine grandchildren, and three great-grandchildren all continue working the family farm, which has now grown to well over 3000 acres across four counties. And the old John Deere "D"? It was restored to new condition in 2001 and began traveling to numerous tractor shows all across Southern Indiana.

Yes, that's quite a story for one old tractor. But shoot, that's nothing really...most old tractors have more than their share of stories to tell. Those old pieces of ageless iron that most of us rural folks cling to have a long history of service to humanity. Old tractors: No country Christmas would be complete without them.

Bein' Country

Wally and Maynard

Howdy! My name is Wally P. Hoglash. The P stands for Percival, which was my momma's daddy's name. I growed up on Hog Ridge which is sitiated exactly two hollers over from the town of Laconia, Indiana. The thing that I want to let you know right from the get-go is that we is country folk. My momma and daddy wuz country folk just the same as all of their kin before them. Now, we is proud to be from the country and I don't give two hoots and a holler if'n you think we's all a bunch of redneck hicks, cause we are and we is damn proud of that fact! The country is the best place in the world to be born and growed up and I ain't never had any itch to go live in the city. I guess if'n you wuz raised in the city it'd be alright, but for an old country boy like me, puttin' me in the city would be like tryin' to wedge a square peg into a round hole-you might get it in there but before too long, it's gonna come right back out!

Now, I have knowed Uncle Bill Hornickel since we wuz both knee-high to a piss-ants. Me and him growed up in the same part of Boone Township, right there on Hogridge Road and I used go over and work on his daddy's farm when I wuz a young feller. Sometimes we'd go fishin' or squirrel huntin' after we finish workin' on the farm and we'd roam these hills all over. Yeah, me and Uncle Bill wuz just like cousins 'cept he wuz a bit more high falutin' than me cause some of his family had that college schoolin' and I did good just to get through high school. Boy, I tell ya, I sure did have me some fun in high school…that wuz the best seven years of my life!

Anyways, I hadn't seen ol' Uncle Bill in a while and no too long ago, I runned in to him over at the Laconia General Store and he tells me that he is a writin' one of them thar books. He askted me if I'd be favorable to writin' some stuff down so he could put it is his book and told him that I wasn't no writer! He sed that wuz ok cause sometimes people like readin' bout someone who is simple like myself. Well, I tolt him that maybe the folks would like readin' some of the letters that me and my friend, Maynard Goodin, write

120

back and forth to one another.

Now, when I wuz growin' up there on Hog Ridge, my best friend in this whole world wuz a feller by the name of Maynard T. Goodin. I don't have any idea what the "T" stands for cause he never tolt me and I never askted. Maynard growed up over on Lamb Ridge which is exactly one holler to the east from Hog Ridge. Maynard wuz somthin' of a black sheep in his family cause his daddy wuz from the city and all of his daddy's kin wuz city folks, too. In fact, Maynard's daddy wuz a highly educated man. He went to one of those big universities and got himself a college degree! Then he got a job a workin' for a big company that built big factories whare they make lectricity. He was travelin' out cheer one time and his car runned out of gas late at night and he walked to the nearest farm house. The old feller thar sed he didn't have any gas that he could give him and they wouldn't be able to git any til the next mornin' so he tolt him he could spend the night in the barn.

Maynard's daddy went out thar and found him a place up in the hayloft to bed down. Well, as it happened, that old farmer had a teenage daughter who wuz about seven-eighths wildcat and in the middle of the night, she snucked out to the barn and climbed right up in that hayloft with him! The next mornin' at about 4 a.m. that old farmer went out to the barn to do the milkin' and caught them two sleepin' up in that hayloft wearin' nothin' but smiles! Well, it goes without sayin' that they had a good ol' fashion shotgun weddin' right after the milkin' got finished and the breakfast dishes wuz all warshed up.

Anyways, nine months later, out popped Maynard T. Goodin! Like I sed, Maynard wuz somthin' of a black sheep in his family cause his daddy's people were all soapfisticated city folks so they didn't think none too highly of Maynard cause of his momma's upbringin'. And his momma's family didn't hold much regard for him neither cause of his daddy's soapfisticated, big city roots.

Maynard's daddy liked the country so much that he builted them a house right thar on the farm where Maynard's momma had lived. So Maynard growed up right out cheer in the country and when we wuz around seven years old, we became friends.

We wuz in the same Sunday school class and one Sunday my

cousin, Elwood Hoglash, sneaked his pet groundhog into the Sunday School classroom underneath his Sunday goin'-to-church coat. We wuz all sittin' at a big table drawnin' pictures of Jesus a walkin' on warter when that groundhog got loose and decided to run up Elmira Winders dress lookin' for a place to hide. Well, Elmira thought it wuz Maynard a grabbin' at her underpants under the table and she stabbed him right in the arm with a big grade school pencil. Maynard always did have a big vocabulary for his age and he hollered out, "Holy Shit!"

Our Sunday school teacher, Miss Pearl, she ran up behind Maynard and smacked him on his neck with a big yard stick and yelled, "You little bastard! We don't use that kind of language in the House of the Lord!"

I looked up at Miss Pearl and sed, "I didn't know we wuz in the Lord's House...I thought this wuz the Old Ladies Aid Hall?" Well, that must have made Miss Pearl even madder cause her eyes got all red and bulgy and she began to shake liken she was a goin' to explode.

In the midst of all of that commotion, that groundhog got all excited and it hauled off and bit Elmira right on her woo-hoo. She fell down on the floor and screamed out, "Miss Pearl! Miss Pearl! Somethin' has me by the pootie-tang!" Well, I always wuz a curious kind of young'un so while Elmira wuz layin' thar on the floor a screamin', I jumped down thar and lifted her dress up so I could see what in the hell wuz a goin' on. The next thing I knowed, Miss Pearl had me by the back of my neck with one hand and Maynard by his neck with the other a draggin' us out into the yard by the Ladies Aid Hall whare she proceeded to take a stick and beat the both of us on our backs sides whilst a screamin' that she wuzn't gonna put up with two little, foul-mouthed perverts in her Sunday School class! Then she made us sit out thar on a stump and pray to Jesus for forgiveness so we wouldn't end up in Hell with thorns in our peckers. At least that what *she sed* wuz gonna happen to us.

Anyways, that is how I became friends with Maynard T. Goodin. We sat out thar on that stump and prayed to Jesus and then we got to talkin' about how funny Elmira looked with that groundhog a hanging on her panties right thar in the middle of the Sunday school class. We both laughed so hard that we forgot all about Miss Pearl. She had come back out to check on us to see if we wuz still a prayin' to Jesus. Well, when she slipped around the corner and heard us both a laughin', she grabbed that stick up and began beatin' on us again.

About that time, my cousin, Elwood, snuck up behind her holdin' that damned groundhog, who wuz purdy pissed off by now, and shoved it right on her big rear end. That groundhog clamped down right on her butt and she screamed out as loud as I have ever heard, "Jesus Christ! Somethin' has me by the ass!" Well, she fell down and wuz a writhin' round on the ground and a screamin'. When she hit the dirt, that ground hog took off into the weeds behind the Ladies Aid Hall like a bat out of hell. Just then, the whole congregation came a pourin out of the church to see what in the hell wuz a goin' on.

The preacher came runnin' over to Miss Pearl to help her up and she looked at us and pointed and sez, "Reverend, these two little sons-a-bitches need to be beat within an inch of their lives!"

Well, Miss Pearl never did return as our Sunday school teacher. Some folks sed that the last they'd heard, Miss Pearl wuz workin' in Louisville at a pickle factory as a brine taster. Anyways, that is the story of how me and Maynard T. Goodin became the best of friends. I'd always figured Maynard would move to the city someday cause he wuz always a saying how soapfisticated them city folks wuz and he'd like to be soapfisticated, too. So, after we gradiated from high school, he up and moved off to Chicago and became a real city-slicker, just like Oliver Wendell Douglass on our favorite TV show, *Green Acres*. Well, anyways, I thought I'd include a letter that I wrote to Maynard, so maybe you folks out there could get to know him a bit better.

Dear Maynard,

I am writing this letter kind of slow cause I know you can't read real fast. Ha Ha! Big Mike over at the feed mill told me to say that...I don't know why but he said you'd think it was funny. He also told me to asked you if you'd been to any of them strip clubs up thar in the big city. I told him that I'd bet you had since you always wuz the best tobacco stripper in all of Harrison County. Maynard, I didn't know they even raised tobacco up thar in the city? That is what we should have cheer in Laconia is a strip club. Maybe then they wouldn't have made us stop raising tobacco if we'd had our own club for the strippers.

Old Chet sed to ask you if you had any dirty girlfriends at those strip clubs. I told him I'd imagine so unless they know how to strip tobacco in the big city without gettin' their hands all gummy. Well, if you do have any girlfriends up there with gummy hands, remember that kerosene will take that tobacco gum right off with no problem. Of course, I'd bet all of them strip club girls up thar in Chicago know all about that kind of stuff.

Oh, I almost forgot to tell you that your Aunt Bessie is finally gettin' married! I know we wuz all kind of worried that she'd never find her a feller but she is a marryin' that new preacher from over at Antioch. She took a shine to him right after he came cheer this past June. She finally got up the nerve to ask him over to her house for supper one Friday evening. Me and Raymond Watts wuz a going frog giggin' back in her pond when we walked past her house that Friday night and we could hear 'em in thar in her livin' room. They must have been a prayin' or something cause she was a hollerin' "Oh, Jesus! Oh, Jesus!" over and over at the top of her lungs and I tolt Raymond that maybe we should go in and check on 'em, but he sed he figured that everything wuz ok. He sed she wuz probably just gettin' some of that old time religion. I seen her the next day and askted her if she and her new preacher friend had a revival on Friday night. She sed she wuz definitely revived. She sed it wuz more like the second comin'. Anyways, they are a gettin' hitched next month. I told Raymond that preacher wuzn't much for a long courtship and Raymond sed, "Well son, if you're a gettin' the cream, you'd might as well buy the cow." Whatever that means.

Oh, by the way, Grandma Millie has been feelin' poorly. It must be serious cause she has went through about six bottles of that Cure-All Tonic that she bought off of that old Indian who drives that *old Ford station wagon. You remember him, dontcha, Maynard? He's got them funny lookin' blue eyes and has that old coon hound named Nipples. Anyways, he stopped by and she tolt him she wuz feelin' a bit depressed and he solt her a whole case of his famous Cure-All Tonic. It wuz helpin' her cause after the first bottle, she wuz out in the garden in her bloomers just a singin' and dancin'! That didn't last long, though. Now all she wants to do these days is lay around on the couch and sleep. I'll let you know if anything changes.*

I do have a bit of sad news to tell you. My cousin, Lester Hoglash, wuz kilt last week. He and Uncle Benny wuz out a coon huntin' one night and the dogs treed a big ol' sow coon up in the top of a shag bark hickory down thar in White Cap Holler. They tried for several hours to get a clear shot at that big ol' sow when finally Lester decided to climb up the tree and shoot the coon. He worked around in the dark for sometime, climbin' up to the top of that hickory tree and when he finally got all the way to the top and wuz tryin' to get his pistol out of his overalls pocket, he lost his footin' and fell all the way to the ground. Uncle Benny sed he kinda looked like a big white leghorn rooster as he fell cause he wuz a flappin' his arms like he wuz a tryin' to fly. Anyways, Uncle Benny buried next to his momma. He sed Lester wuz always fond of the tit so now he'd be set for eternity.

Well, I guess that's all for now. I know how you big city folks are; always a runnin' around and goin' places, you probably ain't got much time to spend a readin' about us old country folks. Oh, Old Jake up at the IGA Foodliner sez to watch out for those fast women up there in Chicago. I tolt Old Jake not to worry about you, Maynard. I tolt him that you knew better than to walk out in the road whare any cars could hit you. Well, I guess I'll go. See you in the funny papers. Ha Ha. Write whenever you git a chance.

Yours truly,
Wally P. Hoglash

Maynard Writes Home

You know, I wuz just sittin' on the back porch the other day a
lookin' at the newspaper. Boy, the world is sure a confusin' place
these days. I mean, you gots fellers wantin' to marry other
fellers…I mean how in the hell is that supposed to work? You
know, if you want to start raisin' cows and you go out and buy two
bulls, you're gonna be out of the cow business real fast cause
them two bulls ain't gonna give you nothin' but bullshit which is
exactly what I think about all of this fuss over two fellers a gettin'
married. The way I figures it, if they is both dumb enough to want
to marry each other, then they is most likely too stupid to know
what they'd be a missin' if they were to marry a woman!

And I wuz a readin' about these city folks coming out cheer to
the country and startin' up these things called "meth labs." I finally
had to ask Big Mike over at the feed mill if he knew what this
"meth" stuff wuz and he tolt me it wuz this stuff that makes you
high. Boy, city people sure are stupid these days. Whenever I
want to get high, I just out to the barn and climb up in loft and set
for a spell; if you go all the way to the top, it's about 35 feet up and
that is high enuff for me! Big Mike sez that "meth" stuff messes the
kids up. I tolt Big Mike kids today are plenty messed up without
having to take any of that meth.

I was a sittin' on the liar's bench down at the Laconia General
Store the other day when this young feller pulled up in some little
ferren car that sounded just like an old MTD lawn mower with the
muffler blown out. The whole car was a shakin' and boomin' with
this noise that reminded me of the time that Nate Oliver used
dynamite to fish for catfish in Old Man Wiggins' pond. Anyways,
this feller got out of that car and I swear it looked like he had
runned his head into the hardware section of the Home Depot. He
had them little metal nail-lookin' things a stickin' through his
eyebrows, a hog ringy lookin' thing in his nose, and a couple of
rings though his lip. He had these big spools in his ears that looked
like axle bushin's out of a '63 Chevy 1-Ton rear-end. And I guess
he must celebrate Hollerween all year long cause he wuz all
dressed up like one of them thar draculas or somethin'. He came

126

back out of the store and I askted him if he used that meth stuff and he sez he didn't use drugs. And I tolt him that he may want to start cause it could only improve his looks.

And that got me to thinkin' about the time when we wuz 14 or so and we wuz playin' baseball on the school grounds. I got a hit and wuz a runnin' to first when I got my feet dangled up in my overalls and fell down face first and got my nose all full of dirt. My cousin, Buck, came runnin' over and started laughin' his ass off at me. He sedI looked like a dumbass with all of that dirt up my nose. Now, my fallin' down an lookin' like a dumbass wuz a complete accident. This young feller at the general store looked like a dumbass and I am sure that it wuzn't by no accident, unless of course he tripped and fell head first in a nail bucket. It is a strange world we lives in, that's fer sure!

Well, Maynard sent me a letter from the big city and I thought I'd share it with you. That Maynard, he sure has become a real city-slicker up there in Chicago. I sure do miss him. I has been tryin' to convince old Uncle Bill to go with me to Chicago to visit Maynard but he just sez that he doesn't think Chicago is ready for a wild man like me. That Uncle Bill; he sure is a card sometimes. Anyways, cheer is the letter Maynard sent me:

Dear Wally,

How is everything thar in the country? How is Big Mike and all of the guys over at the feed mill? I sure do miss all of those good times we used to have over thar a baggin feed. These city folks jest don't know how to have fun like that , that is fer sure.

The guy who lives in the room next to me askted if I wanted to go with him to a Gentleman's club the other day and I sed it had been a long time since I had gone to a men's meetin' at church so I went with him. Wally, I am cheer to tell you that these big city churches sure are different than the ones back there in the country! When we got to the door, they made us give a donation before we even got to hear the preacher talk.

Wally, I ain't never been to a men's meetin' like this before. Not only do they let women folk in thar, but they let 'em walk around neckked! Well, I have been meanin' to join a church since I got up here in the city, so I figure I'll just join that one. I can't wait to see what the Ladies Aid group does, that's fer sure!

You remember when I was fixin' to come up here and your Uncle Lester tolt me that city folks wuz kinda snooty? Well, it ain't true! Thar is a guy down on the corner who is always askin' me ifen I want to buy some weed. I think that is purty nice of him to try to make me feel at home up here in Chicago. I am kinda confused as to how he knew our place back there has all of them weeds a growin' around the house though.

Boy, some of these city folks do worry about a feller, that's fer sure. Thar is this woman on our street who is always a askin' me if I is lonely. She tolt me that if I gets too lonely to jest come over to her place and she'd make me feel right at home. I tolt her that if'n I did, then her momma would have to be thar cause it jest wouldn't be right to visit her without havin' her momma thar. I guess I'll go sometime cause she says she'd love to have a threesome. I tolt her that's jest how we do things in the country!

Well, that's enuff about me, Wally. I have been wantin to asked you about how things have been a goin' with Elmira Winders. Did you ever get up the nerve to ask Elmira out on a date? If'n you haven't, then you should cause she is probably the purtiest girl in all of Laconia. Of course, she looks jest like her daddy, old Jake Winders, 'cept Old Jake don't fill out a gingham dress like Elmira does. I wuz a thinkin' that ifen you were to ask her out on a date, then maybe you should take her to a church social or somethin'.

I guess you could take her froggin' but you want to be careful and not jump in too fast or she might get to thinkin' that you are wantin' somethin' else. Of course, you wuz always on the wild side so I say that if you want her to fry them frog legs fer you, then go fer it! Jest let me know what happens. And don't do anything that I wouldn't do. The guy I work with at the wharehouse, Smitty, tolt me to tell you that. I ain't sure why. It must be one of those city sayin's.

Well, I guess I'd better be going. I usually take a walk every *evenin' down to the park. There is always somethin' excitin' goin' on here in the city. Last nite I met a feller down there who tolt me to come by tonight and we'd break out some Wild Irish Rose. I don't want to miss that cause you know how much I likes to hear me a good old country song. Tell everyone over at the feed mill that I sed "hey" and make sure to write soon with all of the details of your date with Elmira.*

Your friend,
Maynard Goodin

Of Love and Fishin'

You know, one of the best things about growin' up in the country is goin' to the fishin' hole in the summertime. My grandpa Hoglash wuz always a going fishin' and he even took grandma Hoglash with him sometimes. They wuz always slippin' off to the creek or the pond to fish. Funny thing though... I don't recall them ever catchin' many fish. Once I askted grandpa why he and grandma never had much luck whenever they went fishin' together and he says that t'weren't true. He sed he always got real lucky whenever he took grandma fishin'.

I sed, "Well, I ain't never seen y'all bring home any fish."
He sed, "Boy, you ain't been payin' attention, have you? We didn't take any fishin' poles, neither!" Sometimes, I jest don't understand them older folks.

Another thing about spring is all of them city folks drivin' out here in the country. One time, we wuz all a sittin' on the liar's bench over at the Laconia General Store when this feller came pullin' up in one of them fancy little furren sports cars with no top on it. He sed he wuz lost and could we gives him directions to get back to Louvall.

Ol' Jake Crosier speaks up and sez, "Well, you need to go down the road cheer a piece and take a right at the big old oak tree. You're gonna go about two miles and when you git to a fork in the road, you're gonna want to bear to the right. Now, you're gonna go about four mile and when you see a big old barn with an old International F-12 with one wheel missin' sittin' in front of it, jest take a right. That's all thar is to it. Do think y' got that?"

Well, that feller just shook his head and then took off without even thankin' old Jake. We all went back to talkin' 'bout whare the best mushroomin' woods wuz. About 15 minutes later, cheer came that feller in the little furren car again. He pulled up and yelled at Jake, "Hey! I thought you said those directions would git me back to Louvall? All you did wuz have me drive in a big circle to wind up right back cheer again! What's the big idea of givin' me all of those directions if you knew I'd wind up right back cheer?"

Old Jake jest looked at the feller and sed, "Wellll, I jest wanted to see if'n you could foller simple directions before I went to all of the trouble of tellin' you how to git back to Louvall." Boy! Those city folks can sure be ungrateful to a feller for tryin' to be helpful!

Well, I jest got finished writin' another letter to my old buddy, Maynard, an I though I'd share it with you. As you may remember, Maynard moved up to Chicago a few months back and me and him been writin' to one another every month. He is teachin' me all 'bout city livin' and I'm keepin' him up on all of the news from the country. I sure do miss him. Me and Maynard's jest like brothers…'cept we aint.

Dear Maynard,

How are things a goin' up thar in the big city? I wuz a tellin' our preacher about that new church you went to up thar in Chicago. I tolt him all 'bout the Gentlemen's Club Meetin' that they have and how they let those poor girls who can't afford any clothes in thar so they don't have to sit out on the street in the cold. I tolt him that we should start a Gentleman's Club Meetin' in the basement of the church and he jest broke into a prayer. Then he tolt me to tells you that he thought you needed to find a different church before you wind up on the fast road to Hell. Boy! Those Baptists sure don't want a feller to shop around much when it comes to religion!

Well, I know you're a dying to know about me and Elmira Winders. I finally did ask her out on a date and Maynard, let me tell you…Elmira is one soapfisticated woman! When I tolt her that I wuz goin' to take her to a chicken dinner over at the Antioch church, she jest giggled and sez, "Well, if'n you play your cards right, then maybe later we can go parkin' down by Mo-skeeter Crick and you can get desert!"

Maynard, I wuz tempted to be a little disappointed over the whole thing cause she was jest lyin'. She didn't bring any desert at all! And we never did play any cards! Of course, I ain't complainin' cause she wuz purty apologetic about the whole thing. Like I sez, Elmira is very soapfisticated. When I askted her whare she learned how to act on a date, she sez she had been readin' this magazine called Kosmo Polla Ten at the beauty shop. She sed she had read this article called 50 Ways to Please a Man. Now Maynard, I ain't one to kiss and tell, but I can tell you this: even without any desert, I wuz purty pleased!

Me an Elmira have been seein' quite a bit of each other these days. She sure is fun to be with, that's fer sure. Do you remember that time when you an me an Tom Philpot went fishin' all night down at old man Higgins pond and we slept on the back of your daddy's old Ford flatbed? It wuz that time when we got that jug of strawberry wine from the Blank Sisters over at Lanesville...an we jest fished and hit on that jug of wine all night. Do you remember when I sed that it didn't git any better than this? Well, I havin to admit that spendin' time with Elmira is a whole heck of a lot better than that! Don't git me wrong; being out thar with you guys wuz purty fun but Elmira is a whole lot funner, that's fer sure!

Well, I guess I'd better go. I am supposed to have dinner over at Elmira's this evenin' and I don't want to be late. You take care and don't take any wooden nickels. Big Mike over at the feed mill tolt me to tell you that. That Big Mike, he sure is somethin'. He sez I should git Elmira a Valentine's present from this lady named Victoria. I don't know what all she is a sellin' though cause Big Mike sez it is a secret. I think I am just gonna git her a new fishin' pole. Nothin' sez "I loves you" like a Zebco! Well, got to run. We all miss you some kinda bad. Write soon.

Your friend,
Wally P. Hoglash

Spreadin' the Manure

I have been pretty busy helpin' folks get ready to start plantin' their gardens that I ain't had much time to go mushroomin' or even get to the pond to catch a mess of bluegills. See, when I wuz just a youngun, my old Grandma Hoglash once tolt me that I should go into the fertilizer business cause she sed I wuz real good at spreadin' the manure. Grandma Hoglash wuz a real smart woman cause she wuz right. I go out and clean barns out for some folks and then I sells the manure to other folks for their vegetable and flower gardens. Well, I guess it is true what they sez: One man's shit is 'nuther feller's gold.

I remember one time this feller who moved out cheer to the country from city called me up and sed he wanted a load of manure for his garden. I askted him what kind of plants he wuz a raisin' and he sez they wuz what you call *exotic herbs*. Well, I had never heard of exotic herbs, so I took him a load of pig manure from old man Kelsey's hog house cause everybody knows that pig shit will make jest 'bout anything grow. After I dumped that big load of manure out behind his shed, he askted how much he owed me and I sez "25 dollars." As he wuz a gettin' in his pocket book for my money, he asked me if I got high. I tolt him that the highest I ever got wuz up in the top of our old barn when we put hay in loft. Well, that feller laughed and sez, "No, hick boy...I mean do you like Mary Jane?"

Well, I must have got all red in the face cause this feller laughed and sez, "Yep! I think this old boy would love getting' his hands on old Mary Jane!"

I wuz so embarrassed that I couldn't even talk so I just took the money and started to leave. As I wuz a gettin' into my truck that feller handed me a little plastic bag with some of his dried herbs in it.

He sez, "Here is a little bonus for you. This'll get you were you want to be!" Well, I didn't want this feller to think that I wuz some old dumb county boy, so I just grinned and sez. "Thank you much!" and then I drove off for home. Well, I stopped by my Aunt Mabel's house on my way home cause she knows just about everything and what she don't know she can find out at the beauty shop. She took one sniff of those herbs and sez it wuz probably some of those Mexican spices like they put in chili.

So when I got home, I decided to make a big pot of chili and put them herbs in thar'. I figured that I could invite Mary Jane Brewster over for dinner that evenin' cause she wuz always sayin' that she'd like to find a man who could warm her heart. My Grandpa Hoglash always used to say that the sure way to a woman's heart wuz to git her all hot in her bloomers so I figured my chili would do the trick, 'specially with those Mexican herbs in it. So I fixed that chili up and invited Mary Jane over. When she got thar, I tolt her that I had a surprise for her and I took her to the kitchen where I had the table all set with two bowls of that chili and some hard cider. Well, she tasted that chili and I could tell by her face that she wuz impressed so I tolt her it wuz my special recipe that I called "Mary Jane Chili." Well, we each ended up havin' two bowls and then the most parculiar thang happened. Mary Jane got up and started dancin' around the kitchen and laughin'. She danced off into the front parlor and motioned for me to follow. She wuz just a laughin' and gigglin' and dancin' and then she started to unbutton her dress.

Well, I wuz so shocked that I tripped an fell backerds in the wood box by the stove and then everythin' got real dark and fuzzy. The next thing I knowed, I woked up the next morning out in the yard under the shade tree with my old coon hound, Beauregard. After me and Beauregard both used the tree thar in the front yard, I went into the house but Mary Jane was nowheres to be found. All of her clothes wuz lyin' on the floor in the parlor and that whole pot of chili was missin'. Well, I decided to go look for her but I had to get somethin' to eat first cause I wuz sure feelin' a might hungry. So I fried me up a pound of bacon, a half a dozen eggs, some sausage links, six jumbo hotcakes, and some fried taters with gravy...on the side, of course!

Then, I went out and jumped in my old truck and started into town. Jest as I got to the four-way stop, I noticed that a big crowd of people was a standin' out in front of the Laconia General Store a pointin' upwerds. I stopped my old truck right thar in the street and jumped out cause up thar on the porch roof of the store was Mary Jane Brewster, necked as a jaybird, with my big chili pot on her head singin' *We'll Have a Hot Time in the Old Town Tonight!*

Well, I tell ya, it just got real ugly from thar. Whilst she wuz a dancin' around up thar, Mary Jane lost her footin' and fell head first off of the porch ruff right into the trash barrel by the gas pumps. Her bare ass wuz a stickin' out of that trash barrel when suddenly it sounded like someone blew a horn on a river barge. I guess the impact of fallin' off of that roof must have forced out all of the gas that had gathered in her gut from consumin' that whole pot of chili. At that point, the crowd drew back a considerable distance cause the smell wuz a might powerful. I sure wuz glad that I wuz standing upwind, I can tell you that! About that time, that barrel tipped over and Mary Jane came rollin' out of thar and took off like a bat out of hell a runnin' up the middle of the street, headin' out of town with my chili pot still on her head. She was still a singin' and lettin' one blow with every stride she took. Old Dave at the Laconia General Store sez it sounded like someone blowin' on a tuba in the 4th of July parade! They finally found her that afternoon a lyin' in a hog waller over on Jake Crosier's place. I never did get my damned chili pot back!

Well, I never did ask Mary Jane over again cause I knew that I'd never be able to think of her the same way as I did before. It is really hard to have them lovin' feelin's for a woman who you've a seen runnin' necked up the middle of the street with a chili pot on her head a tootin' like a Jersey cow on fresh grass. I'll tell ya though, I did learn me a very valuable lesson from that whole ordeal: Never mix hard cider with Mary Jane Chili; it just ain't right!

Well, as usual, I thought I'd share with you the letter that I am writin' to my old pal, Maynard. As you remember, Maynard went off to the big city to find his way in the world and me an him been swappin' letters about every month.

Dear Maynard,
   How are things up there in the big city? Big Mike over at the feed mill sez to tell you he sure does miss you coming by every

mornin' to have coffee and tell some stories. He tolt me to ask you if you had been out huntin' any split tail up there in Chicago. Maynard, I didn't know that they even let you do any huntin' up thar in the big city. And to tell you the truth, I ain't never heard of a "split tail" before. Are they any good to eat? Let me know if you get any cause I might be able to come up thar to Chicago for a visit and get me some split tail.

Anyways, I do have some sad news for you. You remember that old feller who lived down by Lemon's Pond over on Buck Creek Road? You know, the old feller who used to make that Magic Youth Elixir for my Aunt Lulu Hoglash? Well, he was kilt in a horrible axident last week. Apparently he was a makin' a big batch of his magic elixir when the whole daggone still just blew plum sky high. They hault him over to the funeral parlor for his baurial. Old Nathan Wiggins who runs the place sed he wouldn't even have to embalm him cause he wuz pickled already.

Oh, I pert neart fergot, I runned into to your cousin, Betsy Goodin last week. She wuz crossing the street down by the post office and the old brakes on my truck jest ain't workin' like they is supposed to and I hit her square in her big behind. Don't you worry none, though…I'm alright but it sure playt hell on the front of my old truck. Your cousin Betsy did git purty pissed at me though cause it did tear a snag in her dress. She wuz a wearin' that red and yellow dress that she got when she wuz a courtin' the Presbyterian preacher last summer. You remember that dress, dontcha? It is the one that lookted like that hot air balloon that crashed in the middle of Jake Sanford's cow pasture a couple of years back. Anyways, old Betsy sure did give me a raft of shit over the whole ordeal. She sed I'd have to pay for her a new dress and I tolt her I didn't think that Louisville Tent and Awning wuz in business anymore so we'd just have to wait until the county fair comes to Corydon and see ifen we could buy her one off of a carny. That Betsy sure is full of herself…and everything else in sight that she can stuff in her mouth!

Well, I guess I'd better go fer now…I know that you big city folks have better things to do than listen to us hillbillies ramble on about life out cheer in the country. You take care and good luck on your split tail huntin'. Let me know how many you get. Oh, I almost forgot…old Charlie Sell wanted me to asked you if you had ever been to one of them girlie clubs. He sez that a feller could probably get laid in one of those places. I tolt Charlie that you had a bed in your room at the boardin' house so you wouldn't need to go to a girlie club to find somethin' lay on. That Charlie…he sure is a card! Well, take care and write soon.

> *Your friend,*
> *Wally P. Hoglash*

Pumpin' Pig Poop

Hey everybody! This here is Wally P. Hoglash again! Boy it has been a hot summer this year. The other day I wuz movin' some calves over to the north pasture cause the summer heat has really played hell on the grass this year. Well, as a result of that, I got a considerable amount of cow shit on my old work boots which really didn't bother me none cause my old tomcat had pissed on the floorboard of my truck a few days ago and the smell of fresh cow crap helped to cover the odor.

Well, I had to run into Corydon to go to my favorite store, Tractor Supply. I'll tells ya, every time I go in there I git a warm feelin' all over. It feels like the time when I wuz fishin' down on Ma-Skeeter Crick and slipped up on Elmira Winders a skinny dippin' in the water hole behind Uncle John Arnold's place. Anyways, I wuz a snoopin' around in the Tractor Supply and I seen that they have this book for sale called *A 101 Uses for Manure*. Now, I ain't much on them thar books but any book about manure has got to be a gooden.

I tell ya, that got me to thinkin' about the time that me an my good friend, Maynard Goodin, wuz pumpin' hog manure out of the pit in Hornickel's big hog house. It must have been 'bout a hunert dergrees out that day and that hog shit wuz kinda green in color. It kinda looked like that Mexican chili that old lady Whoppert made one Christmas. Anyways, we wuz a pumpin' a big load in the honey wagon, which is jest like a big shop vac on wheels, when all of the sudden the suction pipe got clogged up. Well, whenever that would happen, the best way to clear it wuz to put the pump in reverse and let the pressure build up and then open the valve on the honey wagon an let the back pressure blow out the clog. Well, I stepped around to the front of the honey wagon to reverse the pump and Maynard stayed in the hog house by the big manure pit. Whilst I wuz a lettin' the pressure build up, Maynard got to lookin' and he seen what wuz cloggin' the suction pipe. He grabbed that suction pipe up and wuz in the process of pullin' an old feed sack out of the end of it. Jest when he got that suction pipe pulled up to whare he could sees in the end of it real good, I opened up the gate valve on the honey wagon. About 3 hunert gallons of soupy hog shit came a blowin' out right in Maynard's face. When I went back to see if the pipe was clear, Maynard wuz a standin' there with all of that warm, green hog shit a drippin off of him. He kind of looked like that Swamp Thing that we seen one time at the drive-in picture show up in Georgetown.

I sed, "Maynard! Are you alright?"

He kinda looked at me real disgusted and finally he sez, "Yeah, I'm alright. It wuz a damn lucky thing I had my glasses on or else I have hog shit in my eyes. I did have my mouth open when the shit hit!"

I wuz tryin' real hard not to laugh an I askted, "Why in the hell did you have your mouth open, anyways?"

Maynard sez, "Well, I wuz a getting' ready to tell you that I got the clog out when my world just turned to shit!"

Well, I warshed Maynard off with the hose and we went on workin' till close to dark. The next day when I seen Maynard I tolt him agin how sorry I was 'bout the whole thing and he sed it wuz no big deal. And that is when Maynard sed somethin' that wuz so phillersopical that I thought it should be writ down for posturity: *Sometimes you get the shit and sometimes the shit gets you!*

That Maynard- he sure has a way with words.

Now, I know that some folks think that pumpin' manure is probably a nasty job but I'm a tellin' you that I always thought it wuz a real treat cause I got to spend a considerable amount of time with the pigs. Most folks don't know it but pigs is jest about the smartest animal they is. I once knew this feller who had a really smart hog. In fact, this hog wuz somethin' of a local hero.

This old farmer had an runt pig that he raised on a bottle. When the pig got bigger, he jest kept him around with the dogs and cats an he wuz jest another pet on the farm. Well, one night the house catched fire while the old farmer and his wife wuz asleep. That pig bursted out of his pen an rushed into the burnin' house and rescued the old farmer and his wife, draggin' them both out into the yard while the farm dogs jest sat there and watched.

Later that summer, the old farmer wuz out hoein' in the tobacco patch when a big copperhead snake crawled up behind him and wuz a zeroin' in for a strike. Like a flash, that pig raced up out of nowhare, grabbed up the snake and started whippin' it around until it finally broked its neck.

And then, in the winter, that old farmer wuz out cuttin' the ice on the pond so the cows could drink when he broke clean through. Well, that old feller wuz jest about drownded when all of the sudden, that pig went flyin' into the barn and came back out with a rope in his mouth. He jumped into that freezin' pond, swam to the old farmer, gave him one end of the rope, and then climbed back out onto the shore, an then pulled the old feller out of thar.

Well, you know how things go in the country; word got out about this pig a bein' a hero and such. Pretty soon, this pig wuz famous.

Later that spring, I had to go to over to his place to haul some cow shit an when I got out of my truck, that pig came runnin' out and he wuz missin' one whole back leg. I turned to the old farmer who wuz a standin' in front of the barn and askted, "Jake, what the hell happened to your pig's leg?"

That old feller sez, "Wally, I'll tell ya, a pig that good you just can't eat all at once!"

Like I sed, pigs is real smart. And they taste good, too. The way I sees it, they make the perfect companion: smart, faithful, an good fer breakfast!

Well, I jest got another letter from my old pal, Maynard T. Goodin who is still a livin' up thar in the big city of Chicago and so I thought I'd share it with ya.

Dear Wally,

How have you been? I hope you have been doin' ok. I am always a tellin' all of the fellers who work at the wharehouse about you. Elmo sez you sound like one real fly dog, whatever in the hell that means. These city folks sure do have some funny sayins, that's fer sure. Thar is this one feller who is always askin' me if'in I want to go with him to sniff out some booty. I always tells him that I just own one pair of boots and I am always real careful not to step in anything so they won't be so smelly. Then he sed that I should go with him to find some hoes which kinda shocked me cause I ain't seen a garden or tobacco patch the whole time I have been here so I don't have any idea why we need to find some hoes. Well, I'll let you know how it all turns out.

I have been meanin' to askted you if you were still courtin' Elmira Winders? I knows that you've always had a thing for Elmira and I was kinda wonderin' ifen you an Elmira might be thinkin' of getting' hitched? She'd make ya purtty good wife, ifen you askted me. I wuz a tellin' the feller who lives next door to me at the boardin house bout you n Elmira an he askted me what she looked like. Well, I showed him that pitcher of Elmira that I tooken at the church picnic the time that my Uncle Alphonse spiked all of the watermelons with Abe Renfrow's moonshine. That feller took one look at Elmira and sez she had one fine lookin' booty. I tolt him that he musta been lookin' at the pitcher wrong cause Elmira wuzn't even wearing any shoes. Then he askted me ifen you wuz a tappin' that stuff. I tolt him "They ain't no way that my bestest friend, Wally, would ever go a hittin' on no gurl." Well, he jest laffed and sez that I am way to crazy. I tell, Wally, these city folks sure do have a funny way of talkin'. I guess they jest ain't got as much edumacation as we country folks got.

Well, I hopes that you an Elmira do keep a courtin' cause I think she'd make you purty happy. I knows that she can really cook good and I knows how much you like to eat. Well, I guess I'd better go fer now. I'm s'posed to go a pitcher show tonight with a couple of fellers from the wharehouse. They sed I'd really like it cause it wuz a real hot flick, whatever that means. I think it must be a pitcher about moonshiners cause one feller sez it wuz a triple X and that wuz what grandpa used to rite on all of his moonshine jugs so he wouldn't get em cornfused with the drinkin' warter. I'll let you know how it wuz. Make sure to tell all of the fellers over at the feed mill that I says "hey." Write real soon.

Your friend,
Maynard T. Goodin

Back Porch Talkin'

Eatin' Country

Eatin' Country

I grew up on country cooking. I had to; I was born and raised on a farm. I didn't fully understand just how fortunate I was until my teens when I started experiencing non-country cooking. I had probably sampled non-country cuisine as a kid but when you're younger, you just don't notice such things. Food is food. No, at some point I began to notice how some cooking was simply better than other cooking. Now, I realize that there are as many different approaches to cooking as there are cooks out there. I am sure that there are plenty of competent urban cooks that can hold their own in the kitchen, but this isn't just about *who* is cooking; it is also about what they are cooking!

I have been blessed to have lived among some of the best country cooks who ever tied on an apron. I am even more blessed that they made sure to not only feed me but also make sure that I knew a thing or two about fixing these dishes myself. It is one thing to be able to throw a few hotdogs or burgers grill for an afternoon cookout and another to slap 150 pounds of whole hog on an open spit and roast it to mouth watering perfection.

One of the great things about growing up and living on a farm is that there is always a good supply of meat whether it's from the livestock that you raised or from the wild game you've taken. Nothing tastes better than mess of fried squirrel and homemade dumplings with some garden-raised green beans and fresh corn-on-the-cob. Now there's a meal fit for a king! And you don't even have to be celebrating a holiday or special occasion!

Of course, there is nothing quite as satisfying as a big platter of fried ham with real mashed potatoes and red-eye gravy; a mess of fresh cooked greens; and a slice of squash pie, still warm from the oven. These were the kinds of meals that I grew up on and still enjoy to this day.

Down-home country cooking is all about making the ordinary taste out-of-this-world. In the traditional sense, it is about taking what is available and turning it into something that is truly unique and satisfying without spending a lot of money. It would be just as accurate to call down-home country cooking the practical approach to preparing food. Call it what you want to call it; country cooking is good eatin'!

The Eatin' Country recipes that I have included represent a variety of the down-home favorites that I grew up on. I know you're gonna enjoy these dishes just as much I do. From my Grandma Hornickel's zucchini dressing to Aunt Carolyn's cheesy concoction and Grandma Helen's (my mother) fried squirrel & dumpling's to Mother Martha's (Carolyn's mother) persimmon pudding, these recipes will bring the best of country cookin' right into your kitchen and will have you eatin' country in no time!

King of the Grill

There is a phenomenon that takes place any time you put a man in front of a backyard grill. Suddenly, this man who has trouble fixin' a bowl of cold cereal is in an instant turned into Bobby Flay. If you don't know who Bobby Flay is, just watch the Food Network; he's up there with Emeril Lagasse, Paula Dean, and Wolfgang Puck. If you don't know who Wolfgang Puck is, he is the over-the-top, angry chef-to-the-stars; like anyone really gives a hoot in hell who made linguini for Charlie Sheen or veal parmesan for Brad Pitt's birthday celebration.

Apparently, men have a gene that is leftover from the days when fire was first discovered and man decided that meat tasted better cooked than gnawed right off of the wooly mammoth while it grazed in the meadow. It was generally safer, too. Most any man can tell you the exact formula for turning a chunk of raw something into the best meal you have ever let slide across your lips. Aside from the grill, the only other cooking talent that most men possess is making chili, which usually consists of taking all of the hot stuff that he can find, putting it into a big pot, and cooking it for a long damned while.

He becomes an expert at physical science; knowing the exact temperature it takes to sear meat to perfection and will know more about charcoal than old man Kingsford himself. In fact, to hear him talk, he knows more about the science and art of cooking over an open fire than any man alive. And if you ask him from where he gained all of this cooking knowledge, he will turn his head toward you, offer a smug smile and say, "Son, it takes years and years of practice to become a master of grillin'." And this is from a guy who is just 26 years-old. His expertise is not limited to just the act of cooking the meat; he will also become a master of barbeque sauce and of seasonings. He will quickly turn from a kitchen-geek to a grillin'-freak! And do you know what? Most of the time, the results of his barbequing efforts are usually very good. I have attended hundreds of backyard barbeques and cookouts and tasted the work of many self-proclaimed grill masters. Not one man has ever prepared anything over charcoal or flame that I would say was bad or inedible. Of course, some are more practiced at the art of grilling, but I believe it is simply a matter of experience and imagination rather than pure cooking talent.

Take my friend, Clyde Pitts. When we were younger, Clyde was the proclaimed "con-a-sewer" of fine, grilled chicken. He had a secret recipe for a basting sauce that started with a good measure of some alcoholic beverage and a blend of spices that made for some of the best chicken I had ever tasted. In fact, his chicken was so good that I once left the hospital on crutches and filled with Demerol after having emergency surgery just to have a piece of Clyde's Famous Grilled Chicken.

Of course, if you want a more "traditional" grilled chicken flavor, nothing beats the grilled chicken at most any country church dinner. For really tasty, traditional "church barbeque" grilled chicken, baste with a mixture of one part water and one part apple cider vinegar with a stick of melted margarine or butter. Each time you turn the chicken, sprinkle or brush on liberally until cooked thoroughly. Then, pour remaining mixture in an aluminum pan, lay cooked chicken in the pan and cover with aluminum foil. Set the pan on the grill over a very low heat and allow chicken to steam for at least an hour or more. The chicken will be tender, juicy, and flavorful. Make sure you give thanks before you eat. Amen.

I once attended a cookout were the burgers were so juicy and flavorful that they practically melted in your mouth. I just had to ask the guy responsible what he did to make those burgers so tasty. He replied that he blended with the ground beef a mixture of A-1 sauce, Worcestershire sauce, ketchup, and onion soup mix. Then he leaned close to me like he was afraid the FBI might have the grill bugged and whispered, "The real secret is that I mix in a half a pound of whole butter into the burger before I make the patties." Talk about making a cholesterol bomb that could cause your heart to explode right in your chest! No matter; these burgers were the best I have ever tasted!

Hamburgers, hotdogs, bratwurst, ribs, steaks, fish, and even venison; any and all meat will always taste better when it is prepared on the grill. There are as many different methods for preparing good eats from the grill as there are guys (and even gals) who like to fire up the charcoal or light the burners and cook outdoors. Even vegetables taste better when they are cooked on the grill. My cousin, Allison, makes awesome veggie kabobs on the grill, so good that I almost forget there is no meat. I said *almost*.

Of course, one of the most popular grilled dishes and my personal favorite is the "pig-cicle" better known as pork spare ribs. There are two types of pork ribs: side-slab and baby-back. Side-slab ribs are a bit cheaper; however, theses ribs tend to contain more fat and have several sections of "gristle-ribs" running through them. Baby-backs, on the other hand, have less fat and cook a bit faster than side-slab ribs, and they are generally more tender. The only drawback to baby-backs is they usually possess a bit less meat in proportion to the bone. In either case, the real secret to cooking ribs on the grill is time and heat; the more time you can allow the ribs to slow-cook over a low charcoal heat, the more tender and juicy they will be.

As for seasoning, some prefer a dry-rub seasoning while others prefer to baste with a mixture of their favorite barbeque or grilling sauce. There are dozens of dry-rub seasoning blends available and as for barbeque sauce, well, the sky is the limit. Most grocery stores will carry more varieties and flavors of barbeque sauce than Auto Zone has of motor oil. Pay close attention when you're in the sauce aisle at the store; there will almost always be a guy standing there comparing barbeque sauces. It's no big deal; it's just what guys do. However, most grill-masters will make their own seasoning rubs and sauce mixtures. It keeps the mystery of the flavor a true secret and serves as his grillin' signature.

The next time you go to a cookout, seek out the grill and find the master chef. Then sit back and watch him work his grill magic. Don't make fun of his apron or his hat; grill masters are usually very sensitive about their attire. If you do ask him what seasonings he is using or what is in the sauce, don't be surprised if he turns to you with a sly grin and says, "Well, that is a secret. It is my own special recipe. I'd tell you…but then I'd have to kill ya!" That is just how Kings-of-the-Grills are. After all, half of the art of being a master chef is to keep them guessing. Bon appétit!

It's Time to Get Growing!

You know, my favorite thing about winter is that spring will eventually follow. It's not that I dislike winter; I enjoy watching the snow cover up the pastures and fields with a blanket of white. There is just something exciting and invigorating about breathing in the cold, crisp air on a frosty winter morning. My favorite part of winter, however, is when I go to the mail box and another seed catalog has arrived to serve as a reminder that spring is just around the corner and the gardening season is nearly upon us.

If you're like me, you'll sit down with every new seed catalog and look at all of those pictures of big, hearty garden vegetables, dreaming of the day in the coming summer when you can sit down to a meal of sliced tomatoes, steaming ears of sweet corn, and freshly picked green beans! Yes, it is definitely time to begin thinking about the upcoming gardening season, regardless of the time of year.

Hopefully, you put your garden plot "to bed" before the long winter set in; that way, you'll be ready to get those cold crops like cabbage and early peas in the ground as soon as the threat of hard freeze is past. My Grandma Hornickel used to say that the last week of March was the best time to get cabbage plants in the ground and sow early peas. She also liked to plant some early kale and a few turnips at this time as well. Ultimately, it all depends on which planting zone you live in, so check with your local county agent or the Farmer's Almanac for the best planting times for your area.

Of the many early garden crops, my favorite is cabbage. Nothing goes better with grilled chicken in June than a big batch of coleslaw made from freshly cut cabbage from the garden. I prefer my slaw to be cut into fine shreds with carrots and a sweet, green bell pepper or two. There are several distinctly different recipes for slaw, each featuring a different flavor. However, at the heart of every great batch of coleslaw is the sweet, slightly biting, savory taste of cabbage.

Cabbage is one of the oldest garden crops in America and can be credited for helping establish the early colonies. One of the greatest hazards of long, ocean voyages from Europe was the disease known as scurvy, which is caused by a lack of vitamin C in the diet. The lack of refrigeration or vacuum packaging made it difficult to include vitamin-rich vegetables for a three month voyages across the sea. These early voyagers discovered that cabbage could be packed in salt brine in large wooden barrels and safely stored for months in the holds of the ship without loosing its vitamin C content. Each passenger would consume a half of a cup of the preserved cabbage each day to help prevent scurvy from setting in. Cabbage seeds were also brought along on the voyage to provide a fresh supply of cabbage for the return trip. This pickled cabbage in salt brine is what we know as sauerkraut. The name *sauerkraut* comes from the Old German "sauer" which means sour and "kraut" meaning plant. For the record, most country folk refer to it as "sour crout." Of course, we also "warsh" our clothes, change the "oral" in our tractors, and "wrensh" our dishes off in the sink.

There are many different varieties of cabbage available: Early Flat Dutch; Round Stonehead; and Savory Red, just to name a few. Brussels sprouts, broccoli, cauliflower, and kale are all close cousins of the cabbage family. Check with your local greenhouse or garden center for the varieties available in your area. If you plan on making kraut, keep in mind that round head varieties tend to hold more leaf moisture which is essential for making good kraut while flat head varieties produce longer shreds for most coleslaw recipes.

Getting those cabbage plants into the garden early requires a bit of fall preparation. Generally speaking, it is a good idea to turn under the garden in the fall just before winter sets in so that the snow and the freeze can break up the soil naturally while allowing free nitrogen from the snow to soak in. Once spring arrives, it only takes a couple of good, sunny days of moderately warm temperature before the soil can then be readied with the aid of a tiller. However, if you didn't prepare your garden for winter in this manner, you will have to wait until the soil is dry enough to till at least six inches deep to begin planting early crops.

Cabbage prefers a well-drained, slightly sandy soil to allow oxygen penetration to the root system. Plant seedling plants in a row approximately 24 inches apart to allow for leaf spread. The outer leaves will develop and spread out, covering the ground. This helps prevent weeds from growing and will retain moisture in the soil. When planting young plants, dig a small hole approximately 3 inches deep, fill with water and place the seedling in the hole, pulling loose soil around the plant. If possible, transplant seedlings on a cloudy day or a few hours before sunset to prevent scalding and wilting. As plants begin to take root and grow, cultivate lightly and pull soil up around the base of the plants. Fertilize the soil with a water-soluble, homogenous plant food like 12-12-12. Adding Miracle Grow to the transplanting water isn't a bad idea, either. This will help the young cabbage plants establish a hearty root system and begin growing. After plants put out new leaf shoots, cover ground surrounding with a layer of clean, weed-free straw. This will help retain moisture in the soil, inhibit weed growth, and act as a barrier between the outer leaves and the ground as the plants begin to mature.

Throughout the plants growing stage, be on the lookout for pests such as cut worms and leaf aphids. If you start seeing little holes in the leaves, then it is time to apply a pesticide dust or spray such as Sevin or Orthene. Check with your local county agent or garden center for a treatment that will work best in your area.

Once the cabbages reach harvestable size, the fun part begins: preparation and eating! One of my personal favorite cabbage dishes is coleslaw. Every family has a favorite coleslaw recipe that has been handed down from generation to generation. Of course, cooked cabbage can't be beat as an excellent side dish to most country meals. And don't forget the stuffed cabbage rolls! Cabbage is a very versatile and tasty garden vegetable that is easy to grow and even more versatile when it comes time to prepare. I have included a number of down-home recipes for you to try, so get out there in that garden and let's get growing!

Back Porch Talkin'

Tomato Madness

Every year around August gardens everywhere begin to fill with the reds, oranges, and yellows of tomatoes ripening on the vine. That means it is probably time to buy stock in pork bellies as the demand for bacon will likely go through the roof with everyone making those BLT's. Every roadside stand and farmer's market will soon be brimming with baskets and boxes of plump, ripe tomatoes, the premier garden vegetable that is actually a fruit. Don't you hate it when someone says that? Like it really matters, especially when you're eating one!

The tomato has a very unique history (don't we all?) and wasn't always America's most loved garden delight. The earliest mention of the tomato was in 1519 when Cortez discovered tomatoes in central South America growing in Montezuma's gardens. He brought some seeds back to Europe but failed to mention if the red fruits could be eaten, so they were raised as ornamentals. Somewhere in the mix of things, someone decided that the tomato was actually poisonous and that anyone who ate one would keel over dead. Of course, these were the same Europeans who decided that smoking tobacco was good for a person because it cleared the head and improved digestion.

In 1808, Colonel Robert Gibbon Johnson of New Jersey brought the tomato to the United States. Again, people feared eating the red fruit because the tart juice just had to be poisonous. This from the same people who didn't have enough common sense to put the outhouse a good distance from their water supply; I often wonder just *how* the United States became the most technologically advanced society in the world?

On September 26, 1820, Col. Johnson decided to prove to the world just how wrong they had been about the tomato. He stood on the courthouse steps and consumed an entire basket of tomatoes while a crowd of over 2000 people watched in anticipation of getting to see the good Colonel drop dead right there on the courthouse steps. The fireman's band even played a mournful tune to add to the excitement of watching this old fool commit public suicide. And people think that watching NASCAR is stupid!

Well, of course, Colonel Johnson didn't die. At one point though, doctors agreed that the tomato could cause stomach cancer because the skin would stick to the walls of the stomach. Of course, modern medicine today agrees that the tomato, which contains lycopene, is beneficial in the *prevention* of cancer. I did have a tomato give me a really bad bruise on my shoulder once, but that was because my friend, Terryl Kron, hit me with a slightly green tomato during a tomato fight in the tobacco patch while we were *supposed* to be cutting tobacco. I am probably one of only a handful of people who can say they were hit by a ninety-five mile-an-hour, fast-tomato! They wanted Terryl to pitch in the minor leagues but he went to work for the government instead. Go figure!

By the mid 1800's, the tomato was a part of American food culture and eventually helped to make one man rich. In 1897, Joseph Campbell introduced a new soup, Condensed Tomato Bisque. It was a move that helped to make him a millionaire *and* a household name. The tomato also proved to be financially beneficial for a few other folks like J. R. Heinz, Del Monte, and the Hunt Brothers.

Today, tomatoes are one of the most popular of all garden goodies and are used to make everything from ketchup and salsa to spaghetti sauce and pizza. With a little care and preparation, fresh tomatoes can be enjoyed long after the frost and cold weather makes going out to the garden to grab a few for a salad impossible. Green and pink fruits can be harvested just before the killing frost and individually wrapped in newspaper and stored at a slightly cool room temperature until they have ripened. My mom once prepared some in this fashion and we had fresh tomatoes until Christmas day!

If you decide to can tomatoes to enjoy throughout the year, make sure to first wash the fruit and remove the stems. Dip into boiling water for a minute or so to loosen the skin. Once the skin has been removed, leave whole, halve, or quarter. Pack into jars, add 1 tsp of canning salt, and add boiling water to cover. Secure lids according to directions and then bring water bath to a boil for 45 minutes. Remove from heat and allow to cool and seal. Then store in a cool, dark place, preferably on a lower shelf. These tomatoes can be eaten right out of the jar or used in any of your favorite dishes. I like using canned tomatoes to prepare minute steaks and tomatoes.

The tomato is technically a fruit because it is an ever-bearing plant; it can even be used to make jelly and even ice cream! I am not sure why Baskin-Robbins hasn't added tomato to its list of 31 wonderful flavors, but for those of you who want to try something different, here is a recipe for tomato ice cream:

Ingredients:
16 ounces of fresh tomato juice, strained
16 ounces of whole cream
3 egg yolks
1-1/2 cups of sugar
3 tsp. Thai Sweet Chili sauce

Pour the tomato juice into a large saucepan and heat to simmering point. Allow to simmer until it has reduced to half of its original volume. Once the juice has reduced, place in a cooled container and place in the freezer until cold (if it is too warm it may curdle the egg yolks). While the juice is cooling, place the egg yolks, cream, castor sugar and chili sauce into a glass bowl and whisk until thickened and almost white in color. Set aside in the fridge until ready. Once cooled, pour tomato juice into the egg mixture and lightly whisk to combine. Pour into the ice cream machine. Process as you would any other homemade ice cream. Serve with a sweet pepper jelly as a topping sauce.

Potatoes & Onions

If you grew up in the country, then you know something about potatoes or "taters" as most country folk call them. In fact, most rural families of the past considered potatoes as a staple food because they were cheap to raise, easy to store for use all year, and could be used in a wide variety of dishes. During the 1940's, most rural families planted at least an acre or more of potatoes each year that would provide enough to be used in meals almost every day.

The history of the potato has been so closely linked to the people of Ireland that most believe that the potato originated on the Irish Isle. However, it has its roots, so to speak, in the Andes Mountains of South America. Over 7000 years ago, the pre-Columbian farmers cultivated the potato and were impressed with its storage quality and its nutritional value. It was only when the Spanish Conquistadors discovered this unusual food crop being cultivated that the Europeans learned about this root-like vegetable that is actual a member of the tuber family. Around 1570, it was introduced to the European Continent, though the Europeans considered it an "underclass food" and used it to feed the poor and prisoners from battle.

Around 1780, the people of Ireland recognized the potatoes' value as a staple food crop. It thrived in the Irish climate, was high in nutritional value, and 10 people could be sustained for a year on one acre of potatoes. By the mid-1800's, the State of Ireland became so dependant on the potato as a principle food source that the failure of the crop from a devastating blight caused a nation-wide famine that cut the Irish population nearly in half from death and forced emigration.

As thousands of Irish fled to the United States, they were happy to find that the potato had already been introduced to the North American continent. German, French, and Polish settlers had brought the potato with them from Europe and had found the climate in the northern half of the United States favorable for production. By the beginning of the Twentieth Century, the potato had become a staple in the American diet and was served in nearly every culture and region of the United States.

To steal a line from Forrest Gump's friend, Bubba, potatoes are like the fruit of the soil. You can bake 'em, boil 'em, broil 'em, grill 'em, fry 'em, and sauté 'em. You can make potato soup, potato salad, mashed potatoes, hash brown potatoes, and French fries. There's potatoes and cabbage; potatoes and turnips; potatoes and shrimp (Bubba's favorite); potatoes and green beans; and potatoes and onions. You can use them in stews, soups, breads, omelets, and burritos. And those sneaky Russians even learned how to use them to make vodka. Yes, the potato is an extremely versatile garden offering.

Potatoes require a bit of manual labor to raise. First, select seed potatoes that will suit you usage needs. Kennebec, Cobbler, Yukon Gold, and Red Pontiac are the popular varieties in our area. Till the soil deep and make sure you incorporate several hundred pounds of organic material or composted manure per 50 foot row. If using a commercial fertilizer, use a low nitrogen number such as 6-24-24 or 5-10-15. Cut potatoes into pieces about the size of an egg and soak in a solution of 2 tablespoons of bleach per gallon of water. Then allow cuts to heal in the sunny area for a few days to let the wounds glaze over. Plant with skin side up in a 6 inch furrow spaced about 12-15 inches in rows 24 to 36 inch apart. Cover lightly with about 3 to 4 inches of loose soil. Once shoots begin to come through the surface, cover liberally with at least 12 inches of a chopped mixture of lightly composted straw and organic mulch. Keep free of weeds and grass. After potatoes have bloomed and are beginning to drop foliage, dig on a dry day so potatoes can be left lying on the top of ground to air cure. After a few days, gather potatoes and store in a dark, cool, dry place in baskets or wooden bins. Many people have luck using dry oat straw as packing/filler in the potato storage box or basket.

The onion, on-the-other-hand, can trace its roots to all corners of the world. Onions were cultivated in ancient Greece and were considered a food of both the poor and of the Gods. Archeologists have discovered onions buried with the Pharaohs with inscriptions that the layers of the onion represented eternal life. The onion, though nutritious and healthful, gained popularity in rural America as a flavor enhancer in the kitchen. Adding a diced onion to vegetable soup or ham hocks and beans helps to bring out the flavor while adding its own unique flavor to the mix. Though it was not typically used as a "staple food," the onion has recently become one of the most popular of garden vegetables. Today, the onion ranks third in popularity at grocery stores and produce markets behind tomatoes and potatoes.

When settlers first arrived on the North American continent, they discovered the onion growing wild. The Native Americans cultivated wild onions and garlic, using both for medicinal purposes. Indeed, the high sulfur content, which gives them a pungent odor, and the high acidity were good for treating wounds to prevent infection. During the American Civil War, General Ulysses S. Grant demanded that the War Department keep his troops supplied with onions to use as wound healers.

By the mid-1920's, most gardens throughout America produced a hearty supply of onions. They are adaptive to nearly every soil type and climate region in the United States. They are easy to grow, easy to store, and can be used in hundreds of dishes to add flavor and dimension. Onions contain water soluble iron, selenium, and vitamin K which helps maintain strong heart muscle and promote the replenishment of red blood cells. Today, most every kitchen relies on the onion as flavor enhancer and a spice. Because the onion is recognized world-wide, nearly every food uses it to add flavor and zest. Think about it: Would White Castles be as popular today if they weren't steamed on a bed of onions? Me thinks not!

There are three basic varieties of onions with hundreds of hybrids of available depending on the climate in your region and the soil conditions in which they are to be grown. The heartiest, easy-to-grow is the yellow standard. These onions are small-to-medium in size, tough-skinned, pungent in odor, sharp in taste, and store very well. Though typically a bit too strong to be eaten raw, they are an excellent choice for cooking into sauces, casseroles, and with meats.

The white onion varieties are milder tasting though it doesn't store as well as its yellow cousin. They require a slightly sandy, well-drained soil that is rich with organic material. The skins are much thinner and tender. Because they are lower in acidic juices and possess fewer tough layers of outer skin, these onions, though sweeter in taste, are a bit more difficult to maintain in the garden because they require more attention than do other varieties.

The purple onion is the mildest of all of onion varieties when it comes to taste and can grow as large as softballs. These have soft skins that easily bruise and are much more susceptible to blight and disease than the other varieties. They make excellent salad onions and are a good choice to slice on a hamburger or just eat raw. They require a soil that is rich with organic material and nutrients. They like a slightly cooler climate and need a steady supply of water.

Onions are usually raised from slips which are available from most seed catalogues. Till soil at least six inches deep, making sure that there is plenty of organic material (composted manure, peat, or pre-bagged potting soil). Plant slips an inch deep every 8 inches apart in a 24 inch-wide bed. After the plants have doubled in height, mulch lightly with either composited straw or a commercial black mulch.

Once the onions have reached maturity, the tops should be broken over to allow plants to mature and harden before pulling. After the onions have hardened in the soil, they can be pulled and laid on screen wire frames to dry for several days. The long, leathery stem tops can then be braided together and hung in a cool, dry place to cure for storage. After curing into late-fall, remove from braided bundle and store in boxes, individually wrapping in newspaper. Average storage life: 6 months or longer.

When I was kid, my Aunt Betty was the onion nut in our family. It was her regular habit to eat onions like most folks would eat apples; whole with a sprinkle of salt. Perhaps this is where I developed my affection for onion sandwiches, which are made by piling sliced onions on a slice of bread, adding salt and pepper, smothering with yellow mustard, and then covering with another slice of bread. Yummy!

And of course, onions and taters go well together. Cut up 6 to 8 medium potatoes into ¾ inch dices. Dice 1 large onion. Place both in an 8 qt. kettle and cover with water. Bring to boil; then reduce heat and simmer for 20 minutes. Add 1 stick of butter and 4 cups of whole milk; salt and pepper to taste and then allow to simmer for 20 additional minutes. There's nothing better on a cold day than good, old-fashion potato soup!

For a special treat, add a cup of crumbled bacon and a can of creamed corn to the soup before you allow it to simmer. Nothing makes tater soup squeal like corn-fed pork!

Corn! Corn! Corn!

Boy! I sure do enjoy that fresh corn-on-the-cob from the garden! Of course, the fresh sweet corn from the garden is long gone by now, but that doesn't change the fact that I sure do enjoy sittin' down to a big plate full of fresh sweet corn. If you hunt around a bit, I'll bet you can still find some fresh produce markets that are still bringing in some late season sweet corn from way down south. It may not be as good as what you raised in your own garden, but it'll still help cure your craving for corn-on-the-cob.

Of course, "sweet corn" is something that the horticulturalists of the twentieth century came up with to create a new produce crop to feed the masses. Prior to the introduction of a hybrid sweet corn, most folks just had to wait until the field corn was in the right stage of growth to go out and bring some in to the house for a special meal treat. Early farm families knew that ears of corn gathered when the kernels were still in the soft, milky-stage were especially tasty cooked right over an open flame on a hearth or on top of the traditional wood cook-stove. The shucks were pulled back and the silks removed and then shucks pulled back over the ear. Most would soak the ears in cool, spring water to let the shucks soak up as much moisture as possible before putting the corn over the fire. This process allowed the water in the shucks steam the kernels until they changed color and firmed up a bit. Then, you could pull back the shucks to form a handle to hold the ear by, smear on some fresh butter or bacon grease, and go to town! This how table corn on the cob became known as "roasting ears."

History tells us that the Native Americans are actually responsible for introducing corn or maize to the world. According to Indian lore, corn originated from the South American continent and was brought to North America by the early tribes of the central plains area. From there, it spread to the east, north, south, and west. The Native Americans say that know one really knows how corn came to be; they say it just came from the sky, a gift from the Creator. For over 1000 years, corn has been cultivated by man and carried forth each year, making it the oldest, continuously cultivated crop in America. Indian legend has it that the Creator arranged a Treaty between the Human Beings and Corn. Each had to depend on the other for survival and to this day, corn doesn't grow wild anywhere; the Human Beings have to plant the corn each year for it to feed the Human Beings. If people were to stop raising corn, there would be massive world hunger and the human race would soon perish. Or I suppose they could just go to McDonald's for a Big Mac and some fries.

For hundreds of years, the Native Americans planted corn, beans, and squash together and referred to them as The Three Sisters. The corn provided a stalk for the bean vines to climb and the beans returned the favor by providing nitrogen to the soil for the corn to feed on. The squash would spread its broad leaves out on the ground and keep the weeds and pest plants from growing and crowding out the corn and the beans. The Indians used this as a model for teaching peace and harmony among all people. At least until the Europeans showed up and taught the Indians a new way to live: Forget peace and harmony. Only the strongest will survive. This, of course, was a lie; it was more like only the sneaky and under-handed will survive, which described those pesky Europeans to a letter.

From the early 1700's to the present, corn has become the dominate crop in American agriculture, surpassing wheat in economic and nutritional value. It is commercially grown in every state in the United States including Alaska and Hawaii. Today, corn grown in America is primarily used for livestock feed and ethanol production; however, the United States also produces nearly seventy-five percent of the corn raised for human consumption.

Most of the corn that is raised for canning and freezing is the result of over a hundred years of horticultural research and development to create a corn that is sweeter and higher in sugary carbohydrates that regular field corn. Recent developments in hybrid sweet corn have produced varieties of "super sweets" that contain extreme levels of sugar, resulting in a deliciously sweet table corn that is excellent for canning and freezing. Of course, there are a few varieties of a regular sweet corn that have been around for over fifty years like NK199 and the all-white kernelled, Silver Queen.

Over the years, corn has proven to be very versatile in numerous recipes. For example, the next time you make a batch of cornbread, dump a can of creamed corn into the batter before baking to add some flavor and texture. Another great way to enjoy fresh corn from the garden is to cut the kernels from the cob and fry in a skillet with bacon grease, chopped onion, and bacon crumbles. And for those who enjoy making salsa from all of those tomatoes you've raised, add some cooked sweet corn to your favorite salsa recipe. Of course, nothing beats good ol' corn-on-the-cob, fresh from the garden and served steaming hot. Bacon grease or butter is your option.

Of course, one other variety of corn is popcorn. Indiana ranks number one in popcorn production, thanks in part to Orville Redenbacher of Tipton, Indiana who helped to popularize the modern popcorn industry during the 1970's. Nothing goes better with a good movie than a bowl of freshly popped popcorn with plenty of butter and salt seasoning. During the Christmas season, nothing says rural Americana better than a tree decorated with stringed popcorn. And don't forget about those old-time sweet-treats, popcorn balls.

So, when you see those big combines chewing their way through a golden field of corn each fall, take a moment and give thanks to all of those who have continuously planted and harvested corn to make it our number one crop in America. It is truly the most versatile food crop in the world today. And it makes for a colorful, tasty addition to the dinner table any time of the year. Besides, it is so daggone much fun to eat right off of the cob!

Vegetable Dishes

Dandelion & Poke Greens

Pick only young, tender dandelion or poke greens.
2 tbs bacon grease
1 tsp Garlic Powder
1 small yellow onion-diced
1-4oz can sliced mushrooms
1 tbs apple cider vinegar
pinch salt

After picking greens, wash thoroughly by dousing up and down in ice cold water. Place greens in large pot, covering with 1-2 inches of water with pinch of salt.
Cook greens until tender, adding water as necessary.
Once tender, add bacon grease, garlic powder, mushrooms, and onion.
Reduce heat and simmer 30- 45 minutes.
Sprinkle with apple cider vinegar before serving.

Aunt Carolyn's Eggplant French Fries

1 large, firm purple eggplant
1 tsp salt
2 tbs seasoned salt
1 cup milk
2 cups self-rising flour
1 tsp pepper
3 eggs
1½ cups Crisco shortening

In a flat dish sift together dry ingredients. Set aside.
In a large bowl beat eggs and milk together. Set aside.
Wash and peel skin from eggplant, starting at the blossom end (the bottom).
Cut eggplant lengthwise into ¼ inch slices. Then cut slices into ¼ inch strips. Place strips into egg/milk mixture, covering them completely. Let stand.
In large skillet, melt Crisco and heat over medium heat.
Dredge coated eggplant strips in flour mixture.

Test oil in skillet by dropping in a pinch of flour, when the flour sizzles; it's ready.
Fry floured eggplant strips in oil for 2 minutes on each side.
Do not overcook.
Remove fried eggplants strips from skillet. Drain on paper towels.
Sprinkle while hot with grated Parmesan Cheese.

Cucumbers in Sauce

3 medium cucumbers
¼ tsp salt
pinch black pepper

½ cup heavy cream
¼ cup vinegar
1 quart iced water

Peel, slice, and chop cucumbers. Place in glass bowl.
Add ice water and pinch of salt.
Cover with plastic wrap and refrigerate for 1 hour.
Beat heavy cream to a thick consistency.
Add salt, vinegar, and pepper. Stir well.
Remove cucumbers from refrigerator and drain well. Cucumbers should be nice & crisp.
Add cucumbers to cream sauce.
Serve with your favorite seafood dish.

Baked Green Beans

2-14.5 oz cans sliced green beans-well drained
1-10.75 oz can condensed tomato soup
½ cup brown sugar
1 medium white onion-chopped
4 slices bacon-cut into 1" pieces.

Preheat oven to 300 Degrees
In square glass baking dish, combine green beans, tomato soup and brown sugar. Blend well.
In medium skillet fry bacon pieces and chopped onion together until onion are translucent.
Pour fried bacon pieces and chopped onions over green bean mixture.
Bake for 2 hours.

Green Tomato Pie

4-6 large green tomatoes	2 unbaked pastry crusts
1½ cups sugar	½ tsp cinnamon
¼ tsp salt	5 tbs lemon juice
5 tsp grated lemon rind	2 tbs butter

Preheat Oven to 350 Degrees

Spray pie baking dish with cooking spray.
Place 1 unbaked pastry crust in bottom of pie pan.
Wash and thinly slice tomatoes. Set aside.
Mix together all other ingredients in a small bowl.
Arrange a layer tomato slices in bottom of unbaked pie shell.
Sprinkle layer with sugar/lemon mixture.
Continue creating layers until pie shell is full.
Top the layers with the other unbaked pastry crust.
Seal edges with a fork by pressing fork into the pie shells
creating a nice rippled edge.
Prick top pastry with fork to allow air to vent.
Bake in oven for 35 to 40 minutes until golden brown.

BPT's Carrot Casserole

16 carrots, sliced 1/8-14 inch thick (about 8 cups)	
¼ cup margarine or butter	¼ cup all-purpose flour
2 tbs minced dried onions	1 tsp salt
½ tsp dry mustard	¼ tsp celery salt
1/8 tsp pepper	2 cups milk
¼ Cup dry bread crumbs	cooking spray
8 oz shredded sharp cheddar cheese	

Preheat Oven to 350 Degrees.
Lightly spray a square glass casserole dish with cooking spray.
In a large saucepan, cook carrots in small amount of boiling water,
covered for 7 to 10 minutes or until tender. Drain.
Meanwhile, in a medium saucepan, melt margarine or butter. Stir
in flour, onion, salt, mustard, celery salt & pepper. Add milk.
Cook over medium heat, stirring constantly until mixture is thick &

bubbly. Remove from heat.
Place half of carrots into prepared dish. Cover with half of
shredded cheese. Repeat with remaining carrots and cheese.
Pour sauce over all. Sprinkle with bread crumbs.
Bake for 20 -25 minutes or until heated thoroughly.

Christmas Puffed Potatoes

4-6 large Idaho baking potatoes-peeled & cubed ¼ in. pieces
1 can Milnot Milk   ½ stick melted butter
salt & pepper to taste   1/3 cup chopped Pimento
parsley sprigs for garnish

Preheat oven to 400 Degrees.
Place potatoes in large kettle and cover with 2 inches of water.
Bring to a boil over medium heat and cook until dry, be careful not
to let the potatoes burn.   Mash potatoes until light and fluffy.
Fold in Milnot milk and melted butter into mashed potatoes.
Coat the sides of a medium size casserole dish with butter.
Carefully turn mashed potatoes into casserole dish. Do not flatten
or spread. Bake for 15-25 minutes.   Potatoes will puff up.
Remove from oven and garnish with pimento and parsley for the
perfect Christmas mashed potatoes.

Stuffed Eggplant

1 large eggplant   2 tomatoes
1 tbs minced onion   1 small green pepper diced
1 tsp salt   ¼ tsp pepper
1/8 tsp celery salt   1 cup minced ham
1 cup garlic croutons   2 tbs melted butter

Preheat Oven to 350 degrees
Wash eggplant. Cut off stem end. Cut lengthwise into two halves.
Remove seeds. Carefully cut out flesh leaving an ¼ inch shell.
Place eggplant shells into bowl of cool water with a pinch of salt.
Meanwhile, chop scooped-out eggplant finely, add salt, pepper

and celery salt.
Add tomato, onion, and diced green pepper to eggplant.
Cook egg plant mixture over low to medium heat until tender.
Remove from heat and add minced ham.
Remove eggplant shells from water, drain and pat dry with a paper towel.
Fill eggplant shells with eggplant and ham mixture.
Crush garlic croutons slightly and toss with melted butter.
Sprinkle croutons on top of prepared eggplant shells.
Bake in glass casserole dish for 30 minutes.

Orange Yamoree

8 large sweet potatoes
1 tbs cornstarch
½ cup brown sugar
4 tsp grated orange rind
1 cup orange juice
½ cup unsalted peanuts-chopped
cooking spray

6 navel oranges
½ tsp salt
¼ cup sugar
4 tsp melted butter

Preheat oven to 350 Degrees
Wash sweet potatoes. Place whole into large pot cover with 3" of water and cook until tender. Remove sweet potatoes from water. Drain and remove skins. Slice lengthwise into 1/4" slices.
While sweet potatoes are cooking. Mix together cornstarch, salt, brown sugar, sugar, grated orange rind, butter and orange juice. Place in medium saucepan. Cook over low heat until thicken.
Peel oranges, removing as much white skin as possible. Do not separate into sections. Slice oranges cross-ways, like a tomato.
Lightly spray the bottom of a 13 x 9 glass casserole dish with cooking spray.
Place a layer sliced sweet potatoes in bottom of casserole dish. Cover with a layer of sliced oranges. Pour thicken orange sauce over layers. Repeat as necessary to fill dish. Top layers with peanuts.
Bake for 1 hour or until lightly browned.

Cabbage-Spaghetti Cheese Bake

1 medium head white cabbage
1 cup broken spaghetti-1 " pieces
1 ½ tbs bacon grease
1 ½ tbs flour
1 cup milk
8 oz package shredded cheddar cheese
¾ cup bread crumbs lightly coated with melted butter
cooking spray

Preheat oven to 350 Degrees.
Lightly spray a square glass baking dish with cooking spray.
Wash cabbage and remove outer leaves, then shred cabbage.
Cook spaghetti in boiling water until tender, but not quite done.
Drain.
Create alternate thin layers of shredded cabbage and spaghetti in prepared glass baking dish.
In non-stick sauce pan, combine bacon grease, flour, milk, and cheese.
Cook over medium heat, stirring constantly until cheese melts and mixture is smooth.
Pour over layered cabbage and spaghetti.
Sprinkle buttered bread crumbs on top.
Cover with aluminum foil.
Bake for 25 minutes.
Remove from oven to remove foil, then return to oven for an additional 15 minutes to brown crumbs.
Let stand 10-15 minutes before serving.

BPT's Ultimate Cheesy Potatoes

10-12 large baking potatoes
1 large white onion-diced
1 ½ lbs Velveeta Cheese, cut into 1/2" cubes
1 lb thin sliced bacon
½ cup sour cream
1 cup Hellmann's Mayonnaise
1/2 cup chives
salt & pepper to taste

Preheat oven to 350 degrees.

Lightly coat a 13 x 9 glass casserole dish with cooking spray. Set aside.
Peel & cube potatoes, place potatoes in a large cooking pot, covering with 2" water, add a hefty pinch of salt. Bring to a boil, reduce heat and continue cooking until almost fork tender. Drain. Do not fully cook.
While potatoes are boiling, in a large skillet, fry bacon until crisp, remove bacon from drippings, drain on paper towels & set aside. Lower heat, add diced onion to bacon grease & simmer until translucent.
In a large 10-12 quart mixing bowl add Velveeta cubes, cooked onion and bacon grease, cooked potatoes, sour cream, mayonnaise and chives. Mix and fold all ingredients together until smooth and slightly chunky.
Add salt & pepper to taste.
Spread potato mixture into prepared casserole dish.
Place dish on a rectangular cookie sheet.
Place dish and cookie sheet in pre-heated oven and bake for 30-35 minutes or until golden brown and cheese is bubbling.
Remove from oven.
Crumble fried bacon, sprinkle on top of potatoes, then press bacon slightly into the baked potato dish. Be careful, it will be hot!
Let stand 10-15 minutes before serving.

Stuffed Onions

6 medium Vidalia onions
1-4oz can mushroom pieces and stems-diced into small pieces.
¼ cup light cream   ½ lb hamburger
½ cup fine bread crumbs   ¼ tsp salt
¼ tsp pepper   1/8 tsp celery salt
¼ cup melted butter for basting

Preheat Oven to 325 Degrees
Prepare onions by slicing off the top slightly, removing loose, dried outer layers and leaving a touch skin layer attached.

Steam onions in a colander placed in a kettle that has 2-3 inches of boiling water until almost tender. About 10-15 minutes. Just enough to loosen the skin between the layers.
Remove onions and let cool. Remove center of onion without disturbing outer shell. Chop up onion center.
In medium skillet, fry chopped onion centers with the mushrooms, hamburger, salt, pepper and celery salt until crumbly. Drain well.
Add bread crumbs and cream to hamburger mixture. Mix well.
Stuff onion shells with hamburger mixture. Place in a buttered baking dish. Bake for 20 minutes, basting with melted butter.

Grandma's Zucchini Dressing

6 cups zucchini-peeled & shredded
1 medium onion- finely diced
1 ½ cups shredded cheddar cheese
1/3 cup cooking oil
1 ½ cups of Bisquick

1 tsp salt
1 tsp pepper
2 eggs-beaten
4 tbs ground sage

Pre-heat oven to 350 degrees.

Mix zucchini, onion, and cheese. Add eggs, pepper, sage, salt, mixing thoroughly. Stir in Bisquick, Pour into a greased 9 X 13 glass baking dish. Bake for 1 hour

Alice's Easy Broccoli Casserole

5 cups broccoli florets
2 cups shredded cheddar cheese
1 medium onion-grated
1-10oz can of condensed mushroom soup
½ cup Miracle Whip Salad Dressing
½ cup whole milk
1 ¼ cup Ritz Crackers-crumbled

1 tsp salt
1tsp pepper
2 eggs-beaten

Preheat oven to 350 degrees.

Place broccoli florets in a pan and cover with water. Boil until tender but not mushy. Drain in a colander.
Combine eggs, Miracle Whip, mushroom soup, and milk. Add half (1 cup) of cheddar cheese, onion, salt, and pepper. Mix thoroughly.
Coat a 9 X 13 glass baking dish with cooking spray. Spread 1 cup of Ritz crumbles in the bottom of dish. Evenly arrange cooked broccoli florets onto of Ritz crumbles. Pour above mixture over top of broccoli, spreading for even coverage. Spread remaining cup of cheddar cheese over top. Garnish with remaining ¼ cup of cracker crumbles. Bake for 45 minutes. Let stand for 10 minutes before serving.

Hot Slaw

1 large head white cabbage	2 tbs butter
4 egg yolks-well beaten	½ tsp salt
1 cup milk	½ cup white vinegar

Finely shred cabbage in large bowl. Cover with iced water for one hour to crisp.
Heat egg yolks, milk, butter, and salt to a slow simmering boil. Remove from heat. Stir in vinegar. Let cool slightly
Drain water from cabbage.
Pour egg/milk mixture over cabbage.
Mix well then serve while warm.

Grandma Hornickel's Hot Skillet Slaw

1 large head white cabbage	10-12 slices bacon
2 tbs Salt	½ cup sugar
1 tsp Pepper	1/3 cup apple cider vinegar

Shred cabbage in large bowl. Cover with iced water for one hour to crisp. Drain well.

In large, deep skillet, fry bacon until crisp.
Lower heat. Remove bacon. Reserve bacon grease in skillet.
Drain and crumble bacon.
To well-drained cabbage, add sugar, salt and pepper.
Tossing cabbage shreds well to coat thoroughly.
Turn heat back up on large, deep skillet.
Add vinegar and bacon crumbles. Stirring well.
Add prepared cabbage shreds to vinegar and bacon in skillet.
Tossing cabbage in skillet until well coated. Do not let cabbage wilt.
Remove from heat and place in large serving dish.

Breads & Biscuits

Baked Cheese Layers

12 slices of bread
celery salt
8 oz shredded cheddar cheese
2-6 oz cans Dawn's Mushroom Sauce
1 cup milk
cooking spray

yellow mustard
paprika
3 eggs-well beaten

Preheat oven to 350 Degrees
Lightly coat square glass casserole dish with cooking spray.
Lightly spread each piece of bread with yellow mustard and
sprinkle with celery salt and paprika.
Layer the casserole dish with 4 slices of bread of prepared bread,
then shredded cheese. Repeat, then place final 4 slices of
prepared bread on top.
In medium mixing bowl, combine eggs, mushroom sauce and milk.
Mix until smooth and creamy. Pour egg mixture over bread layers.
Let stand 15 minutes then bake for 50 minutes.

Cheese Straws

1 cup grated American cheese
1 tsp baking powder
1/4 tsp paprika
2 tbs milk

1 cup flour
½ tsp salt
1 well-beaten egg
cooking spray

Preheat oven to 400 Degrees
In large bowl mix sift together cheese, flour, baking powder, salt
and paprika.
Mix together beaten egg and milk.
Add egg mixture to dry ingredients just enough to make a stiff
dough.
Roll out dough onto a floured board approximately 1/8 inch thick.
Cut into strips 4-5 inches long, 1/4 inch wide.
Twist strips. Place strips onto lightly greased cookie sheet.
Bake about 10 minutes or until lightly browned.

Country Cream Biscuits

2 beaten eggs	1/3 cup cream
4 tbs butter	2 tbs sugar
2 cups flour	4 tsp baking powder
¼ tsp salt	

Preheat oven: 350 Degrees
In large bowl sift together flour, baking powder, salt and sugar.
Add butter, beaten eggs, and cream.
Fold all ingredients together to form a dough.
Place dough on floured cutting board.
Roll out to ¼" thickness. Cut dough with biscuit cutter.
Sprinkle each biscuit with granulated sugar.
Bake in preheated oven for 20-25 minutes until tops are golden brown.

Steamed Brown Bread

1 ½ cups sour milk	4 tsp butter or bacon grease
¾ cup molasses	1 cup chopped raisins
1 ½ cups flour	2 tsp baking powder
1 cup yellow corn meal	1 cup whole wheat flour
½ tsp baking soda	1 tsp salt

In large bowl, mix all ingredients together, thoroughly to form dough, shape into an oval ball, place dough ball into a steam basket. Steam for 3 hours.
In place of steam basket, use a metal colander placed inside a large pot so handles of colander hang over edge of pot with 2-3 inches of water in bottom of pot to steam bread. Do not let water touch colander or dough.

Glazed Spudnuts

2 large potatoes	1/3 cup butter
½ cup sugar	2 eggs-well beaten
1 ½ cups scalded milk	2 packs yeast
2 tbs warm water	1 tsp salt
4 ½-to-5 cups sifted flour	½ tsp vanilla

Prepare deep fryer with fresh Crisco shortening.
Heat to 450-500 degrees.

Wash and peel potatoes. Cut into 1" cubes. Place in kettle, covering with 2" water. Boil until dry.
Be careful not to let the potatoes burn. Mash potatoes in large mixing bowl.
Add to potatoes, butter, sugar, eggs, and scalded milk.
Dissolve yeast in warm water. Add to potato mixture.
Add salt and vanilla.
Fold in sifted flour-one cup at a time- slowly until a light and fluffy dough is made.
Cover with towel and let rise to double size.
Work down and let rise again.
Roll out on floured cutting board. Cut into round shapes. Move to floured wax paper surface and let rise again.
Deep fry in hot melted Crisco.
While still hot, dip into following glaze, then let drain on a shallow wire rack with paper towels underneath.

Glaze
1 lb powdered sugar
1 tbs butter
1 tsp vanilla
1 tbs cornstarch
1 tbs sweet cream
1 tsp warm water
Mix all ingredients together in a deep bowl. While spudnuts are still hot. Completely submerge spudnuts into glaze. Then drain on wire racks with paper towels underneath.

Pecan Crullers

¼ cup Crisco shortening   1 cup sugar
2 eggs-well beaten   3 ½ tsp baking powder
¼ tsp nutmeg   ½ tsp salt
4 cups flour   1 cup milk
2 oz Pecan chips   powder sugar

Prepare deep fryer. Heat oil to 375 Degrees
In large mixing bowl sift together 1 cup of flour, baking powder, nutmeg, and salt. Set aside.
In medium mixing bowl, cream together shortening, sugar, and eggs.
Add creamed sugar and eggs to sifted flour mixture.
Add pecans.
Alternatively add milk and additional flour a little at a time until a stiff dough is formed.
Roll dough out on floured board to ½ " thickness.
Cut dough into 1" x 8" strips. Twist dough strips.
Drop into deep fryer. Do not over crowd.
Fry until golden brown. Drain on paper towels.
When slightly cooled, roll in powder sugar.

Pineapple Butterscotch Biscuit Squares

2 packs dried yeast   ½ cup warm water
1 tbs salt   ¼ cup sugar
¼ cup butter   2 egg-well beaten
5 ½ cups flour
1-16 oz can crushed pineapple; drained-reserve juice

Preheat oven to 400 Degrees
In small bowl combine dried yeast and warm water. Mix well. Set aside.
Add enough water to drained pineapple juice to make 1 cup liquid.
Heat liquid in small saucepan to boiling.
Add salt, sugar, and butter to boiling liquid. Let cool to lukewarm.
Add eggs to dissolved yeast. Mix well.
In large, greased mixing bowl, combine pineapple liquid and yeast/egg mixture to 2 cups of flour.

Beating all ingredients well together.

Add remaining flour-one cup at a time-slowly to make a soft dough.
Fold in 1/2 of the drained, crushed pineapple.
Cover with towel and let chill in refrigerator for 3 hours.

Filling:

2 cups brown sugar	1 cup butter
2 cups flour	remaining pineapple

Cream brown sugar with butter. Add flour and pineapple. Set aside.
Remove dough from refrigerator. Turn dough out onto floured board and cut in half. Roll each half of dough about 1/2" thick.
Spread half of filling onto one piece of dough, then cover with the other piece. Cut into 2" squares.
Generously grease two 9 x 9 baking pans with butter, coating all sides and bottom. Arrange prepared squares, sides touching in baking pans. Cover with remaining filling.
Let stand in baking bans until dough rises lightly.
Bake 25-30 minutes.

Whipped Cream Waffles with Homemade Maple Syrup

1 cup whipping cream	2/3 cup flour
2 eggs separated	1 tsp baking powder
pinch salt	

Beat egg whites until peaks form. Set aside.
Whip cream until stiff, fold in sifted flour, salt and baking powder.
Add beaten egg yolks. Fold in egg whites.
Pour batter into preheated, hot waffle iron. Serve immediately with homemade maple syrup below made at least 1-2 days before serving waffles.

Homemade Maple Syrup
3 ½ cups brown sugar
2 cups boiling water
1 tsp Maple flavoring

Add sugar to boiling water, stirring constantly.
Stir in maple flavoring
Reduce heat, simmer for 10 minutes.   Let slightly cool
Place in a 1 Quart glass jar.
Let stand 24-48 hours. Shake well before serving.

Fruits

Broccoli Strawberry Salad

4 cups broccoli florets	1 cup sliced strawberries
1/3 cup shredded carrots	¼ cup unsalted peanuts
¼ cup red onion-diced small	¼ cup golden raisins

In large mixing bowl, combine all the above ingredients, tossing them well together. Right before serving blend the following ingredients together smoothly and pour over vegetable mixture.

Sauce
¾ cup mayonnaise
2 tbs white vinegar
½ cup powdered sugar

Toss vegetable mixture together with sauce, then fold in sliced strawberries.

Fruit Ice

3 ripe bananas-peeled and mashed
3 oranges-squeezed with pulp
3 lemons-squeezed with pulp
1/3 cup pineapple juice
2 cups sugar
3 cups water

In large glass mixing bowl combine all ingredients. Mixing well by hand.
Pour juice into ice cube trays or silicon molds.
Place in freezer.
Halfway through freezing, place a tooth pick into center of each cube or mode.
Freeze completely.
Use cubes as a natural frozen treat or in a glass of lemonade.

Crystallized Fruit Peels

Fruit rinds- orange, nectarine, lime, lemon, or grapefruit.
(Recipe is enough for 8 pieces of fruit)
2 cups sugar   1 cup boiling water   wax paper

Remove peel from the fruit. Place peels in large pot. Cover with cold water. Bring water to a rolling boil.
Reduce heat and cook peels until soft.
Drain peels in colander.
On wooden cutting board, use the edge of a silver spoon to scrape and remove all white skin from peels.
Cut peels into thin strips.
In a 6 quart kettle, dissolve sugar into water.
Boil to thread stage: When you place a spoon into the mixture and pull the spoon out it forms a thin silver thread.
Add the peel strips. Cook 5 - 8 minutes. Drain. Cool slightly.
Dip in granulated sugar.
Place in single layer on an cookie sheet that has been covered with wax paper.
Let dry 6-8 hours or preferably overnight.
Place candied fruit peels into an airtight container and store in a cool place.

Orange Drops

3 large navel oranges
½ cup powdered sugar
1/8 cup brown sugar
1 ¼ cups flour
1 egg-well beaten
2 tsp baking powder
½ cup milk

Preheat deep fryer to 450-500 degrees.
Use clean white Crisco in deep fryer.
Peel oranges. Remove outer white covering and pull apart into

sections.
Remove skin carefully from each orange section.
Combine powered sugar and brown sugar. Sift thoroughly.
Roll orange sections in sugar mixture.
Mix flour, egg, baking powder, and milk together until smooth.
Dip sugared orange segments into batter.
Drop each orange segment into deep fryer. Do not over load deep fryer.
Deep fry until golden brown.
Drain, then roll or dust with sifted powdered sugar.

Frozen Fruit Salad

5 navel oranges
5 medium bananas
1-8oz can pineapple tidbits-drained
1-8 oz jar Maraschino cherries-drained
1 cup Miracle Whip Salad Dressing
1-16oz tub of Cool Whip-thawed

Peel oranges and bananas.
Section oranges and cut in half.
Slice bananas 1/4 inch thick.
In large bowl, cream salad dressing and thawed cool whip together.
Add all fruits.
Mix all ingredients together.
Coat your favorite mold with non-stick cooking spray.

Spread fruit mixture into mold.
Cover with plastic wrap. Place in freezer.
Freeze 4-6 hours or overnight.
To remove from mold, place mold in a pan of hot water for 30 seconds.

Candy, Cakes & Desserts

Chocolate Corn Flake Mounds

2 squares unsweetened chocolate
1 cup Dates-chopped   ¼ tsp salt
5 cups frosted corn flakes   1 cup pecans
1 lb sweet milk chocolate

Line a large cookie sheet with wax paper.
In large mixing bowl toss together pecans, dates, salt and corn flakes.
In non-stick pan, over medium heat, melt sweet chocolate with unsweetened chocolate squares.
Pour chocolate mixture over corn flake mixture. Evenly coating all ingredients.
Drop from teaspoon in mounds on wax paper. Let cool.
Store in an air tight container.

Chocolate Pecan Toffee

12 Hershey's Milk Chocolate bars   ½ cup butter
1 cup sugar   3 tbs water
1 tsp vanilla   pinch of salt
1 cup pecans-finely chopped

Preheat oven to 275 Degrees
Unwrapped chocolate bars. Lay on wax paper and let stand to room temperature. Close to oven is preferred to soften correctly.
Cover the bottom and sides of a square 9 x 9 shallow baking dish with wax paper; allowing the wax paper to hang over all 4 sides at least 6 inches.
Line the bottom of the baking dish with chocolate bars. Breaking pieces when necessary to completely cover bottom of baking dish. Set aside.
In saucepan, combine butter, sugar, and water.
Cook over medium heat until brown.

Lower heat.
Add vanilla, pinch of salt, and pecans. Stirring quickly.
Immediately cover chocolate bars with hot syrup.
Then cover hot syrup with remaining chocolate bars.
Place in oven for up to 5 minutes to melt chocolate bars together.
Remove from oven.
Let stand on wire rack for 20 minutes.
Fold wax paper over chocolate bars.
Refrigerate 4-6 hours.
Uncover. Place board on top of baking dish. Hold together and flip over.
Remove remaining wax paper. With sharp knife cut into squares.

Cracked Crystal Jewels

1 cup sugar
1/3 cup white corn syrup
1/3 cup water
1 tsp clear vanilla extract or other clear flavoring of choice
small bowl of iced water

Lightly spray a large cookie sheet with cooking spray. Set aside.
In medium non-stick pan, combine all ingredients.
Bring to a boil over medium heat, stirring constantly, until it crackles when dropped into cold water or hard ball stage: **270 degrees.**
Pour mixture into prepared cookie sheet.
Let cool just enough to handle.
Cut candy quickly diagonally in 1" strips-from corner to opposite corner-then turn pan and cut candy again to form diamond shapes.
Candy must be handled quickly as it hardens rapidly.
Remove "diamonds" to wax paper and let cool.
Store in an air tight container.
You may use food coloring of your choice to create a rainbow of crystal jewels. Just add a few drops of your favorite color right before pouring onto cookie sheet.

Orange Nuts

1 ½ cups sugar   ½ cup orange juice
1 tsp grated orange peel   2 cups pecan halves

Line a large cookie sheet with waxed paper.
In medium sauce pan, combine sugar and orange juice.
Cook over medium to high heat, stirring constantly to soft boil
stage: **236 degrees**.
Remove from heat.
Add orange peel and nuts.
Stir gently until syrup becomes cloudy.
Before mixture hardens, drop by spoonfuls onto wax paper.
Cool completely.
Store in air tight container with wax paper between layers to
prevent sticking.

Sour Cream Fudge

2 cups sugar
2 squares semi-sweet chocolate-finely shaved
1 cup thick sour cream
1 tbs butter
1 tsp vanilla
1 cup walnuts-chopped

Coat a 9 x 9 baking dish with butter on bottom and sides. Set
aside.
In a medium, non-stick sauce pan, combine sugar, chocolate, sour
cream, and butter.
Cook over low to medium heat.
Stirring constantly until sugar dissolves.
Boil to a soft ball stage: **236 degrees.**
Remove from heat.
Cool to lukewarm.
Add vanilla and beat until creamy.
Fold in walnuts.
Spread mixture into prepared 9 x 9 baking dish.
Allow to set until completely firm.
Cut into 1" squares.

Tomato Cake with Cream Cheese Glaze

1 cup sugar
2 cups flour
1 tsp baking soda
1 tsp vanilla
1 cup dates-chopped
1-10 ¾ oz can condensed tomato soup

½ cup butter
1 tsp baking powder
1 tsp cinnamon
1 egg-well beaten
½ cup walnuts-chopped

Preheat oven to 350 Degrees

Lightly coat a 8" or 9" loaf pan with Crisco shortening then dust with flour. Set aside.
In medium mixing bowl, cream together sugar and butter.
Add remaining ingredients one at a time.
Mix all ingredients thoroughly together.
Pour mixture into prepared loaf pan.
Bake for 35-45 minutes or until done.
Cool and wire rack for 15 minutes then remove from loaf pan.
Top with cream cheese glaze.

Cream Cheese Glaze

1-6 oz package Philadelphia Cream Cheese-softened
1 cup powder sugar
2 tbs cream
1 tsp vanilla

In small mixing bowl, cream together cream cheese and powdered sugar.
Fold in cream and vanilla.
Mix thoroughly until smooth.
Frost over completely cooled tomato cake.

Orange Sunshine Cake

2 large oranges	1 cup raisins
1/3 cup walnuts	2 cups flour
1 tsp soda	1 tsp salt
1 cup sugar	½ cup Crisco Shortening
2 eggs	1 cup milk
½ tsp lemon extract	1 tsp vanilla

Preheat oven to 350 Degrees.

Prepare a 12"x 12" square cake pan by lightly coating sides and bottom with Crisco. Dust lightly with flour. Invert pan over cake board and tap lightly to remove excess flour. Set aside.
Squeeze 1 large orange, reserving juice from orange in a small bowl.
Remove seeds. Grind the rest of the orange including rind with raisins and walnuts to form a paste.
In medium mixing bowl sift together flour, soda, and salt. Set aside.
In large mixing bowl, cream together sugar and Crisco.
Add creamed sugar mixture to sifted flour, along with the eggs and milk.
Blend well for 2 minutes. Add lemon extract and vanilla.
Mix all ingredients well.
Fold in orange/raisin/walnut paste, again mixing well.
Pour batter into prepared pan and bake for 40-50 minutes.
Remove from oven and place on wire rack to cool for 10-15 minutes.
Invert pan onto a floured cake board. Remove pan by lifting straight up. Place cake on covered cake board or platter.
Slightly pierce cake with fork and drizzle reserved orange juice onto top of cake.
Top cake while still warm with the following topping preparation.

Orange Sunshine Topping

½ cup sugar	1 tsp cinnamon
½ cup walnuts-chopped	1 tbs cream
powder sugar	toothpicks

Combine sugar, cinnamon, and walnuts in medium bowl.
Toss together. Add cream.

Mixing well to coat walnuts with sugar.
Sprinkle over top of warm orange sunshine cake.
Dust top light with powder sugar.
Peel and section 2nd large orange.
Carefully remove outer skin of each section.
Roll each section in powder sugar.
Place a toothpick in the middle of each section then attach orange slices to side of cake, starting with the corners first, then spacing the rest evenly apart on the sides. Reserving two sections to be place on top of cake.

Red Earth Cake

4 tbs cocoa
1 tsp red food coloring
½ cup Crisco Shortening
2 cups flour-well sifted
½ tsp salt
4 tbs 8-hour old coffee-heated to boiling

1 tsp vanilla
1 ½ cups sugar
2 eggs
1 tsp baking soda
1 cup buttermilk

Preheat oven to 300 Degrees

Coat a 12" x 12" x 2" square cake pan on all sides and bottom with Crisco shortening.
Lightly dust pan with flour. Turn pan upside down and tap out excess flour. Set aside.
In small mixing bowl, mix strong coffee, cocoa, and food coloring to form a smooth paste.
In large mixing bowl, cream together sugar and shortening, then fold in eggs.
Sift together flour, baking soda and salt.
Alternatively add sifted flour mixture and buttermilk, a little at a time, to creamed sugar mixture.
Add cocoa paste to bowl and then add vanilla. Mix well until smooth. Pour batter into prepared cake pan. Bake for 30-35 minutes until done.
Let cool on wire rack for 10-15 minutes. Then invert on floured cake board or serving plate. When completely cooled, frost with your favorite frosting.

Rhubarb Upside-Down Cake

3 cups diced rhubarb
10 large marshmallows- cut in half
¾ cup sugar

BATTER

½ cup Crisco Shortening
1 cup sugar
¼ tsp salt
½ cup milk

1 ¾ cups sifted flour
2 eggs
3 tsp baking powder

Preheat oven to 350 Degrees

Prepare a 10" round spring form pan by coating the sides and bottom with shortening then lightly dusting with flour. Invert the pan on a cake board and gently tap the bottom to remove excess flour.
Place diced rhubarb in a single layer in bottom of pan.
Top rhubarb with halved marshmallows.
Sprinkle 3/4 cup sugar over marshmallows and rhubarb.

Prepare batter as follows:
In large mixing bowl, cream together shortening, sugar, and eggs.
Sift together flour, salt, and baking powder.
Add sifted flour mixture to creamed sugar mixture, then add milk.
Pour batter on top of rhubarb.
Bake for 1 hour or until toothpick inserted in middle of cake comes out clean.
Remove from oven. Let stand on wire rack for 10-15 minutes.
Place covered cake board on top of spring form pan. Sandwich the two together and invert.
Remove spring form pan from cake.
Drizzle a glaze over entire cake made up of 2 Cups Powdered Sugar, 1 Tablespoon Vanilla, and just enough milk or cream to create a smooth glaze.
Let stand 15-20 minutes before serving.

Root Beer Cake

2 cups sugar   ¾ cup Crisco Shortening
3 cups flour   2 tsp baking powder
½ tsp salt   7 oz favorite non-diet root beer
5 egg whites-stiffly beaten to form peaks

Preheat oven to 350 Degrees

Coat a 12" round cake pan or two 8" round cakes pans if you want a double layered cake, with Crisco shortening. Dust pans with flour. Turn pans upside down on a cake board and tap bottom lightly to remove excess flour. Set aside.
In large mixing bowl, cream together sugar and shortening. Add flour, baking powder, and salt.
Blend well.
Add 7 oz of your favorite root beer and mix all ingredients well by hand for 1 minute.
Gently fold in stiffly beaten egg whites.
Pour batter into prepared pans.
Bake for 20-25 minutes or until light golden brown and completely done.
Remove from oven and place on wire racks for 10-15 minutes.
Using a cake board or platter dusted with flour, place the cake board over top of cake pan and invert the two.
Remove cake pan and let completely cool before frosting with frosting below.

Root Beer Frosting

2/3 cup water
4 tbs Wilton Meringue Powder
12 cups (3 lbs.) sifted confectioner's sugar (powdered sugar)
1 ¼ cups Crisco Shortening
1 tsp clear vanilla extract
1 tsp root beer extract flavoring

Combine water and meringue powder. Whip at high speed until peaks form. Add 4 cups sugar, on cup at a time while beating at low speed. Alternately, add shortening and remaining sugar. Add flavorings. Continue to beat until smooth. Frost cake as normal.

Butter Pie

1 cup sugar
3 eggs-separated
2 tbs sugar

½ cup pure butter
1 tsp vanilla
1-9" pie shell-unbaked

Preheat oven to 450°

In medium mixing bowl, cream together sugar and butter.
Add egg yolks and vanilla. Mix well.
Pour mixture into unbaked pie shell.
Bake at 450° for 10 minutes.
Reduce oven heat to 350° and bake an additional 25 minutes.
Remove from oven and cool slightly.
In small chilled mixing bowl, combine egg whites and sugar.
Beat until stiff peaks form.
Spread egg whites on top of cooked pie.
Return to oven and brown lightly.

Carrot-Potato Pudding with Froth Sauce

½ cup butter
1 cup peeled carrot-grated
1 ¼ cups flour
½ tsp allspice
1 cup raisins
1 cup chopped figs
1 tsp baking soda-dissolved in small amount of hot water

1 cup sugar
1 cup peeled potato-grated
1 tsp vanilla
1 cup chopped dates
½ cup chopped walnuts

In large mixing bowl, cream butter and sugar together until smooth.
All the rest of the remaining ingredients, one at a time, in order
giving to creamed sugar mixture.
Blend well.
Prepare large double boiler. Steam mixture in double boiler for 3
hours.
Serve with Froth Sauce.

Froth Sauce

1 tbs butter	1 tsp vanilla
1 cup powdered sugar	1 tbs boiling water
2 eggs-separated	½ cup whipping cream

Cream butter, slowly add sugar, beating constantly.
Add well-beaten egg yolks gradually to creamed sugar.
Add vanilla and hot water.
Beat eggs white until stiff peaks form.
Beat whipping cream until firm and smooth.
Slowly fold egg whites into mixture.
Heat over boiling water for five minutes, stirring constantly.
Remove from heat. Fold in whipped cream. Serve while warm
over Carrot-Potato Pudding.

Frozen Nut Pudding with Cream Sauce

8 oz slivered almonds	4 oz chopped walnuts
8 oz candied cherries-sliced	4 oz crushed pineapple-drained
½ cup cooking sherry	1 qt. rich boiled custard
1 qt. heavy sweet cream	½ cup sugar
1 cup shredded coconut	1 tsp vanilla

In large, freezer mixing bowl, blend all ingredients together in order
given. Cover with plastic wrap or lid. Freeze for 4-6 hours or
preferably over night.
Serve with cooled cream sauce.

Cream Sauce

2 egg yolks-well beaten	2 tbs powdered sugar
1 tsp vanilla	1 cup whipped cream

In top double boiler combine eggs and powdered sugar. Stirring
constantly until thicken. Remove from heat, beat until cold. Add
vanilla, then fold in whipped cream.

191

Grandma Martha's Persimmon Puddin'

2 cups persimmon pulp
1 tsp baking soda
1 ½ cups sugar
dash of salt
¼ stick butter/margarine-melted

2 ½ cups all-purpose flour
1 tsp baking powder
1 tsp allspice
1 ½ cups milk
2 eggs-well beaten

Preheat Oven to 325
Lightly coat 9" x 13" baking dish with a thin layer of Crisco, then dust with flour—set aside.
In large mixing bowl, sift together all dry ingredients, set aside.
In medium mixing bowl, beat milk, eggs, and butter.
Add egg mixture to dry ingredients—blend well.
Fold in persimmon pulp until well mixed.
Pour battered into prepared baking dish.
Bake for 45 minutes.
Remove from oven. Let cool for 15 minutes. Serve warm with whipped topping.

Frozen Strawberry Marshmallow Delight

1 pint fresh strawberries
½ cup milk
1 cup whipping cream
cooking spray

½ cup sugar
8 oz miniature marshmallows
3 cups crushed vanilla wafers

Barely coat a 2 quart glass freezer dish with cooking spray. Cover bottom of dish with half of the crushed vanilla wafers. Set aside.
Wash and remove stems from strawberries. Let drain completely.
In medium mixing bowl crush and mash fresh strawberries and sugar together. Set aside.
In a small chilled mixing bowl, beat whipping cream until stiff. Place in refrigerator.
Meanwhile in a non-stick sauce pan add milk and mini marshmallows.

Simmer over low heat until marshmallows are completely dissolved.

Let cool slightly.
Fold melted marshmallows into crushed strawberries.
Gently fold in stiffly whipped cream.
Pour strawberry mixture over crushed vanilla wafers.
Top with remaining crushed vanilla wafers.
Cover tightly.
Freeze 4-6 hours or preferably overnight.

Ice Box Cake

4 tbs sugar	4 tbs water
3 sections semi-sweet chocolate	3 eggs-separated
1 tsp vanilla	30 ladyfingers-separated

Line a 13" x 9" glass baking dish with waxed paper. Layer bottom of glass dish with separated Ladyfingers. Set aside.
Beat 3 egg whites until stiff peaks form. Set aside.
In double boiler bring sugar and water to a boil. Add chocolate pieces. Continue cooking until all chocolate melts.
Remove from water. Let cool slightly.
Add egg yolks to chocolate mixture and beat thoroughly.
Add vanilla.
Slowly fold in egg whites. Blend well.
Pour 1/3 chocolate mixture over ladyfinger layer.
Layer more separated Ladyfingers on top of chocolate mixture.
Coat again with 1/3 chocolate mixture.
Continue with another layer of Ladyfingers and chocolate mixture.
Cover and let stand overnight in refrigerator.
Turn out on to cake board. Remove wax paper and frost with whipped cream.

Martha's Coffee-Can Persimmon Bread

4-1lb metal coffee cans with lids
3 cups sugar
2/3 cup water
3 ½ cups all-purpose flour
1 tsp salt
1 cup chopped walnuts

2 cups persimmon pulp
1 cup Crisco Oil
4 eggs-well beaten
2 tsp baking soda
1 tsp cinnamon
1 tsp Nutmeg

Preheat oven to 350 degrees

Prepare metal coffee cans by lightly coating with shortening and dusting with flour.
Set aside.
In large mixing bowl, cream together sugar, Crisco oil, water, and eggs. Mixing well.
Add dry ingredients one at a time, beginning with sugar and flour.
Then add rest of dry ingredients.
Fold in persimmon pulp. Blend well.
Fill each prepared coffee can half full.
Set up on right on a cookie sheet.
Place in oven without lids and bake for 1 hour.
Leave in can. When completely cool, replace lid, then decorate the can and lid for a nice house warming gift.

White Cloud

5 egg whites
½ tsp cream of tartar
½ pint whipping cream
1 cup shredded coconut

¼ tsp salt
1 ½ cups sugar
1 tbs sugar
cooking spray

Fresh Strawberries or other fresh fruit of choice if desired.

Preheat oven to 450°

Lightly spray an 8"-10" round cake pan with cooking spray. Set aside
In large chilled mixing bowl, beat egg whites with salt until foamy.
Add cream of tartar and continue beating until eggs form stiff peaks.

Gradually add sugar one teaspoon at time to egg whites until no longer sugary or granularly.
Fold in vanilla.
Pour into prepared cake pan.
Place cake pan in oven.
Turn off oven. Do not open door. Leave in oven overnight.
The next morning;
Add whipping cream and sugar together and beat until stiff.
Remove white cloud from oven.
Spread whipped cream over top.
Top with shredded coconut.
Cover loosely and let stand in refrigerator for 4-6 hours.
Serve alone or with your favorite fresh or canned fruit pie filling.

Caramel Peach Pudding

4 ripe peaches-skinned, pitted & halved
¼ cup sugar   1/8 tsp salt
1 tbs flour-heaping   2 ¼ cups milk
2 egg yolks-well beaten ½ tsp vanilla
¾ cup crushed macaroons ½ cup caramel sauce
1 ½ tbs sugar

Prepare double boiler.

In mixing bowl, combine the ¼ cup, flour, salt, and a ¼ cup of milk.
Scald the 2 cups remaining milk, add scalded milk gradually to well-beaten egg yolks.
Slowly add sugar mixture to egg/milk mixture.
Cook in double boiler, stirring constantly until mixture thickens.
When cool add vanilla.
Spread half custard mixture into a square glass casserole dish.
Layer the halved, ripe peaches on top of custard.
Spread remaining custard on top of peaches.
Smooth caramel sauce over top of custard.
Sprinkle top with 1 ½ teaspoons sugar.
Cover & chill in refrigerator 2-4 hours. As caramel stands it will crystallize slightly.

Cake Perfection

Aunt Carolyn was in the wedding cake business for nearly 25 years. She was the preferred wedding cake baker for David's Bridal and a member of Wedding Cakes Across America from 2006-2008. Below are her award-winning secrets for baking the perfect cake every time.

The best cakes are always made two days ahead of when you want to serve them. When planning to bake a cake for a special occasion or anytime, bake the cake two days before and frost it the day before you want to serve it.

Her preferred box cake mix is Pillsbury with pudding in the mix. When baking any type cake whether from scratch or box, lower your oven temperature to 325 degrees and increase your baking time 5-15 minutes depending on the size of the cake pan.

Always use solid Crisco shortening to completely coat sides and bottom of cakes pans. Place Crisco coated pans on stove top while oven is preheating to "liquefy" Crisco and to season cake pans.

Then dust with sifted flour, shaking the pans back and forth, then turning the pans on their sides and rolling them to ensure a good dusting around all the areas.

Turn the pans upside down on a cake board and tap the bottom lightly to remove excess four.

For extra moisture and flavoring in any cake, add 2 teaspoons clear vanilla, 2 tablespoons cooking oil and 1 tablespoon water. This is in addition to any oil, water, or flavorings that the cake recipe calls for.

Do not over beat your cake batter-only mix, blend, or beat cake batter for a maximum of 2 minutes. Always fill your cake pans 2/3 full. Pour batter in center of cake pan, then use back of spatula in middle of cake batter to smooth batter out to the edges.

Do not pick up pans and tap on counter to remove air bubbles. You want the air in your cakes so they will be light and fluffy.

Always test your cake for doneness. Do not rely on a timer. Cakes are completely done with a toothpick inserted in the very center of the cake comes out completely clean or when you touch the center of the cake and it bounces back like a soft sponge.

If the cake is browning faster than getting done, lower the oven temperature 10 degrees and continue baking.

When you remove your cakes from the oven, place them on a 2-3 inch tall wire rack so air can get under the cake pan. Leave on wire rack 10-15 minutes.

Do not let the cake completely cool in the pan.

Prepare three cardboard cake boards bigger than your cake pans by lightly dusting them with sifted flour, if you have only 2 cake pans, if more cake pans are being used always prepare one more cake board than the number of pans used.

Place a floured cake board on top of cake pan, invert the two together, paying attention to supporting the cake pan and board. Place the two on your counter top and tap the bottom on your cake pan to help release the cake from the pan.

Lift the cake pan straight up off the cake. Place another floured cake board on top the cake, invert two again and quickly remove the top cake board.

Place the unfrosted cake layer, now upright on a clean floured cake board, in a kitchen cabinet or cupboard and let stand for 24 hours.

Do all remaining cake layers the same manner and place them together in a kitchen cabinet.

To prepare cakes for frosting, remove one cake layer from cabinet at a time. Cake should look moist and slightly damp on top.

Run you hands over and around the cake still on the board to remove any loose crumbs.

Use a cake leveler to cut off the rounded portion of the top of the cake. Do not cut off an excessive amount. Just trim the round portion off.

Prepare a clean cake board by covering it with colored cake paper or florist foil paper. Place a dab of frosting on the center of the prepared covered board.

To remove cake half from floured cake board. Turn over the prepared covered foiled board and place it on the center the cake that has been leveled.

Invert the two, removing the original floured cake board. You now have the base for your cake.

Take another cake from the cabinet, remove crumbs and level it.

Apply a generous mound of frosting in the center of the base cake with a spatula.

Using a frosting knife that has been "warmed" in a glass of hot water, spread the frosting from the center out to within 1/2" of the cake's edge.

Place the other level cake layer or top cake with the leveled side down to frosting on top of the frosted middle. Gently press the top cake down allowing some frosting to flow out the center.

With "warmed" frosting knife, smooth out any frosting around the center to "glue" the two cake halves together.

Let the cake settle for 15-20 minutes. More frosting may creep out around the center. If so smooth the center frosting again. Apply a very, very thin layer of frosting to the top and sides of your cake. Let stand for 30 minutes to form a crust over entire cake.

To frost the entire cake, apply a mound of frosting to the top of the cake. Again, using a "warmed" frosting knife, spread frosting to the edge of the cake.

Now using the back of your frosting knife, apply frosting to the sides of the cake, turning it as you smooth the frosting around the cake.

Before adding any decorations or boarders, allow the cake to set-up or "crust over" for 30 minutes or so before applying.

Return finished cake to kitchen cabinet or place on a cake stand under glass. By following the above steps, your cake will be moist and flavorful on the inside and picture perfect on the outside.

Meats & Wild Game

Uncle Bill's Mouthwatering Ribs

3 slabs pork ribs-semi frozen
seasoned meat tenderizer
pepper
sea salt
butter spray

Preheat oven to 450 degrees

Remove semi-frozen ribs from package, rinse and pat dry with paper towels. Lay ribs onto counter covered with wax paper. Spray each rib generously with spray butter, then sprinkle a layer of seasoned meat tenderizer on top, followed by sea salt and pepper.
Turn ribs over and prepare other side the same way.
Place ribs in a very large roaster, rib bones down.

Bake as follows:
450 degrees for 15 minutes
400 degrees for 30 minutes
350 degrees for 45 minutes
290 degrees for 1 ½ -2 hours until tender.
Brush on bar-be-que sauce, if desired,30 minutes before ribs are done.

Aunt Carolyn's Swiss Kraut Chicken

3 lbs frozen chicken tenderloins
1 large can of sauerkraut-drained
1-10 ¾ oz can condensed cream of celery soup
1 soup can of milk
1-16 oz package shredded Swiss cheese
1 tsp seasoned meat tenderizer
pepper

Preheat oven to 350 Degrees.
Lightly coat a 13 x 9 glass baking dish with cooking spray.
Layer the bottom of prepared baking dish with drained sauerkraut.
Place frozen chicken tenders on top of sauerkraut.
Sprinkle with seasoned meat tenderizer and pepper.
In small mixing bowl combine cream of celery soup with 1 soup
can of milk. Mix until smooth and creamy.
Pour celery soup over chicken tenders and kraut.
Cover with aluminum foil and bake for 50 minutes to one hour.
Remove from oven.
Spread shredded Swiss cheese on top of chicken tenders.
Return to oven for 15 minutes or until cheese is completely melted
but not browned.
Let stand 15 minutes before serving.

Country Fried Squirrel & Dumplin's

2-3 squirrels-gutted, skinned, and cleaned-cut into pieces, soaked
overnight in cold water with 2 tbs of salt.
1 ½ cups Crisco shortening
2 cups flour
1 tsp meat tenderizer
1 tsp pepper
1 tsp salt
1 small onion- diced
½ cup celery leaves

Remove squirrel pieces from salt water and place into a large pot
of boiling water. Parboil for 25 minutes. Remove from water.
Reserve water for dumplin's.
In a large skillet melt Crisco. While Crisco is melting, mix together
dry ingredients in a large bowl.
Drop squirrel pieces into flour, coating all sides.
Fry squirrel in hot Crisco until gold brown on all sides.
Drain on paper towels.
While squirrel is frying prepare dumplin's as follows:
Mix together 2 cups of flour, 1 tsp salt, dash of pepper, and 1
TBSP baking powder. Add enough cold water to flour mixture to

form stiff dough. Roll dough out onto a flour surface about ¼ inch thick. Dust with flour. Cut dough into 1" x 2" squares.
Add diced medium onion and celery leaves to reserved water.
Bring to a boil. Drop dumplin's one by one into boiling water.
Boil until fluffy -About 10 to 15 minutes. Leave dumplin's in water until ready to serve with fried squirrel.

Baked Rabbit with Wine Sauce

2 Rabbits -skinned, gutted, and cleaned-cut into pieces, soaked overnight in cold water with 2 tbs of salt.
1 ½ cups Crisco shortening
2 cups flour
1 tsp meat tenderizer
1 tsp pepper
1 tsp salt
1 cup semi-dry white wine
1 medium sliced onion
1 ½ cups water

Preheat Oven to 350 Degrees.

In a large bowl, combine all dry ingredients.
Remove rabbit pieces from salt. Dredge wet rabbit pieces into flour, coating all sides.
Fry quickly in hot Crisco searing all on sides.
Drain on paper towels.
Place fried rabbit pieces into a 9" x13" casserole dish.
Cover rabbit with slice onion.
Blend white wine and water together. Pour over rabbit.
Bake for 30 minutes at 350 degrees, then lower heat to 300 degrees and bake for 1 ½ - 2 hours until tender.

Grandma Helen's Steak &
Country Tomato Gravy

1 lb. of tenderized beef round steak, cut into portions
1 cup of flour seasoned with salt, pepper, and meat tenderizer 1 cup of cooking oil
1 medium diced onion
4 medium tomatoes-cut into wedges
½ cup of flour (for gravy)
2 cups cold water
1 cup milk

Preheat large skillet with 1 cup cooking oil.
Dredge steak pieces on both sides in seasoned flour, place in hot oil.
Cook until golden brown on both sides.
Remove from skillet and drain on paper towel.
Place diced onion in hot skillet. Cook until over medium heat until clear.
Remove from skillet.
Using grease and drippings from steak, brown ½ cup of flour in skillet.
Add cold water and milk, stirring until smooth.
Add cooked onions, then place browned steak pieces into skillet with gravy.
Add the tomato wedges and season lightly with salt & pepper.
Cover and reduce heat to a low simmer for twenty minutes.

Aunt Carolyn's Cabbage Casserole

3 lbs. ground beef
1 medium head white cabbage
2 cups instant rice, uncooked
2 -14 oz cans diced tomatoes
1-10 3/4 oz can condensed tomato soup
1-1/2 cans water
Salt and Pepper
Cooking spray

Preheat oven to 375 Degrees

Lightly coat a deep, 13 x 9 glass baking dish with cooking spray. Set aside.
Wash cabbage and remove outer leaves, then finely shred cabbage.
In prepared 13 x 9 glass baking dish, create layers starting with the shredded cabbage, sprinkle uncooked instant rice over cabbage, then add the raw hamburger and tomatoes.
Sprinkling each layer with a dash of salt and pepper.
Add the water to the tomato soup. Stirring until smooth.
Pour tomato soup over layered casserole.
Place casserole dish on cookie sheet and cover with aluminum foil.
Bake 3-4 hours or until cabbage is tender.
Let stand 20 minutes before serving.

Back Porch Talkin' Meat Loaf with Cream Sauce

3 lbs ground smoked ham
3 lbs lean ground hamburger
1 lbs sage sausage
4 eggs-well beaten
1-10 ¾ oz can condensed tomato soup
1 can evaporated milk
1 ½ cups cracker crumbs

Preheat oven to 350°
In large mixing bowl combine ham, hamburger, and sausage. Set aside.
In medium mixing bowl combine eggs, tomato soup and evaporated milk. Mix well using a wire whisk until smooth and creamy.
Add to meat mixture.
Slowly add cracker crumbs. Mix all ingredients together thoroughly.
Form meat mixture into two loaves.
Place loaves into a ungreased, glass baking dish.
Bake for 1 ½ hours to 2 hours until brown and done.
Remove from oven and let stand 10-15 minutes.

Cream Sauce:
1 Pint Whipping Cream
¾ Cup Mayonnaise
½ Cup Horseradish
4 Teaspoons Prepared Mustard
2 Teaspoons Salt
¼ Cup Chopped Parsley

In medium, chilled mixing bowl beat whipping cream until stiff.
Fold in mayonnaise.
Gently add horseradish and mustard.
Fold in salt and parsley.
Chill 10-15 minutes.
Serve as topping for meatloaf.

Country Ham & Cheese Potato Soup

4-6 large Yukon Gold potatoes- cut into 1" pieces
½ cup of *I Can't Believe It's Not Butter*
1 medium white onion-diced
½ cup chopped celery
¼ cup of dried chives
1-12 oz can Carnation Evaporated Milk
12-16 oz of country ham pieces
2 tbs bacon drippings
½ cup instant mashed potato flakes
½ cup finely shredded Colby cheese
1 tbs salt
1 tbs pepper

In large kettle, place potatoes, covering with 4" water. Add margarine, onion, celery, chives, salt, and pepper. Cook, uncovered, over medium-high heat until potatoes are fork tender, but not over done. Do Not Drain.
Reduce heat to low simmer. Add Carnation Milk, country ham, and bacon drippings. Simmer 15 minutes. Slowly add mashed potato flakes while stirring. Then sprinkle cheese on top, slowly stirring in as cheese melts. Reduce to low heat, cover and simmer for 2 hours, stirring occasionally.

Uncle Bill Hornickel

<u>Notes</u>

Back Porch Talkin'

The Tale End

Prose or Poetry

Back in the old days, the small, one-room schools that dotted the rural countryside offered a better education than the big, consolidated schools of today, mostly because the teacher had the chance to spend more time with each student, one-on-one.

My dad went to a small one-room school when he was in the lower grades, what was then referred to as Grammar School. One day they were a sittin' in class and the teacher said, "Ralph, what is the difference between prose and poetry?" And my dad said he didn't know and that kind of made the teacher a bit angry so she went to the chalk board and wrote:

There was an old lady who lived on a hill, and if she isn't dead, she lives there till this day.

The teacher said, "This here is prose cause it doesn't rhyme." Then she wrote:

There was on old lady who lived on the hill, and if she isn't dead, she is living there still.

And then the teacher said, "This is poetry cause it does rhyme." My dad looked at the teacher and he said, "I understand that pretty well."

So the next day when school started she thought she'd test him a bit, so she said, "Ralph, come up to the chalkboard and show the class what you learned yesterday."

So dad went to the board and wrote:

There was a pretty girl, a sweet young lass, she tripped on a rock and fell on her... and then dad looked at the teacher and asked, "Well, what do you want: Prose or poetry?"

Losing Your Mind

For many years, rural folks have known that sometimes when folks get older, they start to actin' a bit crazy and lose their memory. Of course, we now have a fancy term for that called "Alzheimer's Disease."

There were these three old brothers over near Rabbit Hash Ridge who had spent their whole lives farming together. All three were widowed by the time they were sixty and they had never remarried. When they got up in years, their children, who had already taken over the farming operation, had them move into one house together so they could better care for them. Before long, all three began to get extremely forgetful and exhibit erratic behavior. Their kids decided that all three needed to see a doctor to determine if they could continue living together without supervision.

They took them to see a geriatric specialist over in Louisville, Kentucky. He sat all three of them down and said,
"I'm going to give you a little test."

They all nodded and the doctor then asked the first brother, "What is 3 times 3?"
He looked at the doctor and without hesitation replied, "157".

The doctor wrote something down on his clipboard and then looked at the second brother and asked, What is 3 times 3?"
The second brother replied, "Tuesday".

Again, the doctor scribbled on his clipboard and then looked at the third brother and asked, "What is 3 times 3?"
The third brother replied, "9".
The doctor said, "That's right! How did you get the answer?"

The third brother replied, "Well, I took 157 and subtracted that from Tuesday!"

The Language of Love

One of the greatest problems that married couples face is that men and women often speak two completely different languages, which can sometimes make communication a bit difficult. Not too long ago, a preacher friend of mine told me a story about a young couple in his congregation. One evening the husband came home after a long day at work and was greeted by his wife who informed him that she had a bit of trouble with her car.
"What kind of trouble," the husband inquired.
"Well, I'm pretty sure that the darn thing is flooded," she replied.
He nodded and said, "Well, I'll take a look at it after dinner."
Once he had finished eating and had changed into his old clothes, he informed her, "Honey, I am going out to the garage to work on your car."
Bewildered, she looked at him and asked, "Why are you going to the garage?"
The husband replied, "Well, you said it was flooded. I am going to see if I can fix it."
The wife put her hands on her hips and indignantly asked, "Well, don't you think it would be easier to fix if you got it out of the *swimming pool* first?"
In the case of this couple, the word "flooded" held two entirely different meanings.

Love Lessons

A young groom was waitin' out behind the church for his weddin' to begin when his father approached him and said, "Son, while we still have time, you and I need to have a Man-to-Man talk about marital love."
Somewhat embarrassed, the son replied, "Dad! I am 23 year-old college graduate. I pretty much know all there is to know about sex!"
The father shifted nervously and then replied, "Exactly! That is why your mother sent me out here to ask you a few questions!"

Eternal Peace

One thing about rural communities is that there are small cemeteries everywhere. One afternoon, I was walking home from a neighbors farm and I passed by this little cemetery near our place and there was a fellow there standing by a grave and he kept saying in a sad, mournful tone, "Oh, why did you die? Why did you die?"

And it touched my heart, you know, cause this feller seemed to be in so much pain. So I walked over to him and he said it again. "Oh, why did you die? Why did you die?"

So I asked, "Who was it that died? Was it your mother?"

He said, "No, it wasn't my mother. Oh, why did you die? Why did you die?"

I asked, "Was it your father?"

He said, "No, it wasn't my father. Oh, why did you die? Why did you die?"

So I asked, "Was it your brother?"

"No, it tweren't my brother, either. Oh, why did you die? Why did you die?"

So I asked him, "Well, who in the world was it that died?"

He looked up at me with tears in his eyes and said, "My wife's first husband!"

The Order of Things

My Uncle John went into town one day to do his trading. That's what the old country folks used to call goin' shopping. So, he walked downtown to visit with the old fellers who used to hang out at the Liar's Bench. Just then, a funeral procession started passing by. Everybody got quiet, faced the street, and removed their hats.

Uncle John did the same and while they was a standin' there, he whispered to the old boy next to him, "Who died?"

The old guy answered, "The one in the first car!"

211

Wiser Men

My Grandpa Hornickel was a school teacher in a one-room school house over near Glenwood. Back in those days, teachers were allowed to teach about the first Christmas and the birth of the baby Jesus. As always, on the last day before Christmas vacation, my grandpa gave the class a little quiz over everything they had learned about the first Christmas. He would make each student come up and stand in front of the class and he would ask them a question. This was during the Great Depression and times were hard. My grandpa knew that many of his students wouldn't get very much for Christmas so he made the questions easy so that when they answered correctly, he would give them a small gift; a bag with an apple, some peanuts, a couple pieces of hard candy, and a new pencil.

He got to the last student, Johnny, who was a big strappin' 16 year-old boy in the third grade. Johnny was in the habit of not paying attention in class a great deal of time and Grandpa knew this so he wanted to make Johnny's question an easy one so he could give him his Christmas gift.

He asked, "Johnny, what was the occupation of the three Wise Men?"

Johnny shuffled his feet and looked at the ceiling for a long moment while the rest of the class watched and listened nervously.

Finally, he looked at Grandpa and said, "They were firemen!" Grandpa looked at Johnny with disappointment and sighed, "Johnny, why in the world would you say that they were firemen?"

Johnny looked straight at Grandpa and said, "Well, the Bible plainly says that 'they come from a-far'!"

Grandpa gave Johnny his gift.

The following tale was handed down from Carolyn's grandfather, Irvin Ira Sprayberry. As a Native American, he told this story to his children and grandchildren as a way of passing along a bit of Native American heritage while instilling in them to never forget their roots.

Watch For Falling Rock

All of those years ago, when the Pilgrims first landed at Plymouth Rock, they discovered that America was not just an empty wilderness full of natural resources. For reasons I'm sure no one understands, the Pilgrims made the assumption that they were the only humans on this side of the earth for they were surely surprised when they discovered that they were not alone on the North American continent. There was a whole race of people already living here, a race of people who possessed a rich culture and heritage; the Native Americans.

Well, Duh! Chalk one up for the arrogant stupidity of the white man! They came all the way from England to the New World only to find it wasn't really a "new world," that it was, in fact, someone else's "old world." We all know the rest of that story: Because the white men were Christians, they were entitled under "God's authority" to destroy the Native Americans and drive them from their homeland so that they, the white settlers, could build homes, churches, schools, towns, strip malls, large factories, nuclear power plants, and football stadiums. And so, the Native American Indians began their great migration to extinction. Though it took nearly three hundred years, eventually all that was left of the North American Indian Nation was their heritage and a rich past filled with many legends and stories.

One of these stories eventually made it into the culture of the white man; though most of us who are fair skinned have no clue what it means. And so this story begins:

Once, many, many seasons ago, before the white man sailed to this land from far across the great water, there were many Indian Nations all living here in peace. In one particular tribe, the chief had a young, beautiful daughter who was named Black Hair Blowing. When Black Hair Blowing came of age, the chief decided that it was time for her to marry. Since the chief had no sons, he

213

wanted Black Hair Blowing to marry the strongest, wisest, most worthy brave in the tribe so that one day he could become chief. So the old chief went up on a mountain and spent three days and nights trying to decide how to find a brave who was worthy of Black Hair Blowing's hand in marriage. When the chief finally came down from the mountain, he announced that he would have a contest to find the strongest, wisest, most worthy brave in the whole tribe.

The next day, all of the available braves in the tribe were brought together to begin the contest to determine who would marry Black Hair Blowing and become the next chief. The chief told them that they would have to run to the top of the furthest mountain, find an eagle feather and a tortoise shell and bring them to the chief. Only the best eagle feathers and tortoise shells would be accepted. And so, all of the braves, twelve in all, took off running toward the furthest mountain in search of eagle feathers and tortoise shells. It took them nearly three days, but when all twelve had all returned, the chief had each one come forward and present their gifts. Eight braves had beautiful feathers and large, shiny tortoise shells.

The chief turned to these eight braves and said,
"Now, you must go and bring a piece of blue turquoise to make a wedding necklace for Black Hair Blowing. Only the bluest and shiniest stones will be accepted."

And so the braves left, each in search of blue turquoise stones. When at last they returned, the chief had them all come forward and present their gifts. Four braves presented stones that were pale in color and dull in the sunlight; however, the other four braves presented brilliant blue stones that glistened and sparkled in the sun. The chief said to them,
"You four braves have proven yourselves worthy and now must move on to the next test. The great black bear that lives near the foothills of the great mountains had twin cubs last spring. Both of these young bear cubs have an extra claw on the left paw. The first two braves to return with a left bear paw with an extra claw will be deemed as worthy to continue in the contest."

And so, the four braves left for the foothills, each in search of the bears with and extra claw. The very next day, two braves, Wild Deer Standing and Falling Rock returned to the village, each carrying a left bear paw that possessed an extra claw. The chief was very happy, for these two braves were the strongest, wisest, and most worthy. Black Hair Blowing was especially happy because unknown to her father, she was secretly in love with Falling Rock and he was in love with her. She had been secretly cheering for Falling Rock to win so that they could be together forever. Now, only one test remained.

The next day the chief went to Falling Rock and Wild Deer Standing and said to them,

"Now, it is time for the toughest test of all. The first one of you to return with the head and hide of the great white buffalo will win my daughter's hand and will become our next chief. We will all be waiting for your return. Now go!"

And so the two braves left. Many, many weeks went by and neither brave returned. All of the people in the tribe became very anxious and concerned. The old chief began to worry that neither brave would make it back. Black Hair Blowing became very sad for she feared that Falling Rock would never return. Then one day, many seasons after their departure, Wild Deer Standing returned to the village without the head and hide of the great white buffalo. He went to the chief and told him that he had failed the test.

The chief said to Wild Deer Standing, "We have waited many, many days for you and Falling Rock to return. I fear that Falling Rock will never return. I have decided to allow you to marry my daughter even though you did not successfully complete the last task in the contest. Our people will need a new chief soon for I am old and will soon be leaving to walk among the Great Spirits."

Wild Deer Standing told the chief that he was honored but because Falling Rock was his friend, he could not accept the chief's offer until they knew of Falling Rock's fate. The chief hastily agreed and search parties were immediately sent out to find Falling Rock. They searched and searched for many, many seasons. Messengers were sent to the other tribal nations to see if any of them knew of Falling Rock's fate. No one in all of the North American Indian Nation had seen Falling Rock. Generations passed and all of the Indians in all of the tribal nations continued the search for this bravest, wisest, most worthy brave. Then, the white man came and the Indian nations began to disappear. But the few who remain are still looking for this most worthy brave who can become chief and lead the Indian Nations once again.

Today, as you drive down most any road in America, you will see that the Indians are indeed still looking for him for they have put up signs asking you to watch... for Falling Rock.

The Legend of White Cap Hollow

Most tall-tales start with an ounce of truth and end up with a pound of exaggeration. At least that's my observation. The tale of White Cap Hollow has certainly had its share of twists and turns over the years. It goes something like this: Way back in the old days, a few years after the Civil War, Harrison County had the reputation of being a pretty rough place, especially in the southern parts of the county. The close proximity to the Ohio River may have had something to do with this while others blame the ill behavior of southern Harrison Countians on the fact there were so many moonshiners and taverns scattered around this area. Whatever the reason, during the 1800's, vigilante justice reigned in many parts of this area.

Down in Boone Township, just east of Laconia, lived a family by the name of Conrad (pronounced "coon-rod"). *At this point in the story, someone should really start playing a banjo tune.* Now, old man Conrad was a pretty rough character who was known to get into a scrape or two over everything from stealing horses to messin' around with some other feller's woman. As the story goes, old man Conrad got into an argument with a guy from Mauckport over a hand of poker. This fellow pulled a gun on old man Conrad and he pulled his gun in self-defense. Old man Conrad got the drop on him and shot him, graveyard dead. Everyone knew it was in self-defense, but you know how things go in a small town. There was a bunch of guys who thought that since old man Conrad was such a scoundrel anyway, that they'd better take matter into their own hands and go lynch him. What they didn't know was that Old Man Conrad had already been locked up in Kentucky for being drunk and disorderly in a tavern.

This group of vigilantes wanted to disguise themselves so no one would know who they were so they all wore white hoods and robes. They rode through the woods on a moonless trail, up the hollow along Mosquito Creek to where the Conrad family lived, looking to lynch Old Man Conrad. However, before they could get up there, a friend of Old Man Conrad warned his two sons of what was going to happen.

The Conrad boys hid up on the hillsides on either side of the narrow hollow and waited. When the lynch mob, dressed in their white hoods and robes, rode up to the house in the night, Mrs. Conrad came out on the porch and asked them what they wanted. They told her that they came to get her husband and she told them that he wasn't there. Well, since they had come all that way in the dark and they really did want to lynch *somebody*, they asked where her two sons were, figuring that they were probably just as bad as their daddy.

Old Momma Conrad then held her lantern up high over her head so her sons could see the men and yelled out, "They're right behind you! Let 'em have it, boys!"

The boys opened fire and killed several members of this lynch mob. It was total chaos as the "white caps" tried to run back out of there amid the crossfire. The next morning, Mrs. Conrad had her boys go out and drag those dead white caps up into the hollow cause she didn't want dead bodies stinking up the place. Well, instead of burying them, the boys just left them up in the woods for the wolves and coyotes to eat. Somehow word got out that the Conrad boys had murdered several members of a legal posse and that didn't sit well with the county sheriff. Several days later, the boys were arrested and tried before a county jury. They were found guilty and hung off of the West Bridge in Corydon. Old Man Conrad was so pissed that he went back to Kentucky and got into a knife fight with a feller over a lame horse and was killed. Shortly after that, Old Mrs. Conrad came down with the fever and died. A couple months later, the old Conrad cabin burned down in the middle of the night. All that remains to this very day are the old foundation stones where the house once stood.

That is just one version of the story of White Cap Hollow. Over the years, there have been many variations, so many in fact, that no one really knows just exactly what happened up there in those woods. Now, some people claim that to this day, if you're down in White Cap Hollow on a moonless night, you can hear the screams of men and see ghosts dressed in white robes and hoods riding horses down that hollow. Still others claim that if go down there at night and listen real close, you can hear gunfire echoing up and down the hollow.

Of course, you're just as likely to see Burt Reynolds, Ronny Cox, Jon Voight, and Ned Beatty paddling down Mosquito Creek in a canoe (*cue the banjo music again, please*). Well, you know how tall-tales are; some are just ghost stories and some become major motion pictures.

Family Planning

Most farmers look for a wife like they were buyin' a tractor. She has to be dependable, versatile, well-kept, easy to maintain, and forgivable when you screw up.

Raisin' a daughter is like raising hogs: keep them well-fed, healthy, and clean and hopefully someone will take them off of your hands when they are grown.

Never try to teach a pig to sing: It wastes your time and it annoys the pig.

The Buy of a Lifetime

Tractor For Sale: Low hours; fresh paint; 80% rubber on the rear tires; 3-point hitch; dual remotes. Always shedded. Well-kept and in good running condition. Missing the seat and steering wheel. Perfect for the farmer who has lost his ass and has no where to turn! Call BR-549

A Thanksgiving Lesson

Now, we all know the story of the Pilgrims and the first Thanksgiving. Well, at least we *should* know the story. I teach eleventh grade English in a large, urban high school and not long ago, while studying a chapter in the literature book on the journal writings of William Bradford and the Plymouth Bay Colony, I asked my class of seventeen-year-olds to write a short synopsis of the first Thanksgiving. Here is a compilation of how these young folks believe Thanksgiving came about:

During their first year in the new world, the Pilgrims suffered terribly because they weren't prepared. They were running dangerously low on basic supplies like food, toilet paper, firewood, aspirin, deodorant, and soap. Because they were Christians, they really didn't know how to do things like shoot wild animals for food, use animal skins for blankets, or build a bathroom. Just when it looked like they wouldn't make it, two Indians, Pocahontas and Tonto, showed up with some beef jerky, apples, and whiskey to help them survive the winter. When spring finally arrived, more Indians showed up and taught the Pilgrims how to raise food like corn, tobacco, and pumpkins by digging holes in the garden and filling them with dead fish. Later that summer, the Indians held a pow-wow and showed the Pilgrims how to smoke a peace pipe and dance naked around the fire. At first, the Pilgrims were grateful for the Indians showing them that dancing was okay, but then a white preacher gave a sermon about hanging sinners with a grey thread and they all got scared for the Indians to hang around.

After they harvested all of the crops in the fall and saw that they had enough food to make through the next winter, they decided to have a big feast to offer thanks to the Gods for allowing them to make it one year. They sent invitations to the Indian camp because it was the Christian thing to do. On the selected day, they all gathered in the town square and sat down at big, long tables with the Indians to a huge feast that the women folk had prepared. Then, the Pilgrim leader, Captain John Smith, stood up and led everyone in a prayer, including the Indians. When he finished, they feasted on turkey and stuffing, wild venison, sweet potatoes, corn-

on-the-cob, cranberries, beef jerky, and coleslaw. They then offered toasts to each other with apple cider and lemonade. The Indians all got drunk and wanted to fight and the Pilgrims then declared war on them. This is why the white man killed all of the Indians. The Indians ran off into the woods to hide and make things hard for the Pilgrims.

From that day on, the entire world has celebrated Thanksgiving in November. Then, during the Civil War, President Roosevelt had Congress declare Thanksgiving a Federal holiday so that department stores could make extra money during the Great Depression. They called the day after Thanksgiving Black Friday in honor of the Emancipation Proclamation which freed all of the blacks living in America. That is the history of how Thanksgiving began.

Now, if you are sitting in your easy chair that this very moment scratching your head and wondering what part of the above summary is inaccurate, then perhaps you should consider obtaining a library card and spending some quality time reading about American history. On the other hand, ignorance is bliss. Just take comfort in the fact that someday the young folks who were responsible for this Thanksgiving summary will someday soon be running this country. God Bless America!

Chicken Little

There aren't too many old fashion general stores around anymore. You could buy almost anything you needed at these wondrous market places. Nearly every small town had one where you could get everything from a box of corn starch to pound of roofing nails. Most all general stores also had a meat counter where you could grab a pound of boloney, freshly sliced from the roll or some fresh pork chops for dinner. Tom Fink owned one of these stores over near Buena Vista. Folks in that area knew that he would often get special deals on items and they were in the habit of stopping in. Most good general store owners were crafty salesmen and Tom was one of the best. He could sell a blind man a comic book or a drowning man a glass of water.

Early one Saturday morning, Tom drove his old delivery truck into New Albany to pick up supplies at the railroad warehouse, when he noticed that they had a special on fresh, whole chickens. They had them packed in crushed ice in those big, heavy waxed cardboard boxes so Tom figured that he could sell at least two boxes to folks wanting a fresh chicken to fix for Saturday evening dinner. When he got back to his store, he dumped the two boxes of fresh chickens into a big cooler that was right under the meat counter. He made up a sign advertising the special deal and placed out on the front porch of his store. All day long, whenever people would stop in to get a bag of horse and mule feed or a can of coffee, Tom would begin his sales pitch about the great deal he had on fresh, whole chickens back at the meat counter. Tom was a pretty good salesman and he was doing a great job of convincing folks just how much they wanted chicken for supper that evening. By closing time that afternoon, he had sold all but one small frying hen. He had made a pretty good lick of money so he figured he'd take the last hen home and have his wife, Louise, fry it up for dinner.

Just as he was about to close up, a rather primpy old lady from over near the Glennwood neighborhood came pulling up in a big old Buick Coupe. Tom was rather tired, but he was one to never turn away a chance to make a dollar or two so he quickly put his store apron back on and stood ready at the counter when she came walking in.

"What can I get for you this afternoon, young lady," asked Tom. He knew that flattery was a good way to a lady's heart and her pocket book.

She said, "Well, I am having my preacher and his wife over for dinner tomorrow after church and I wanted to get some fresh lamb chops to fix. Do you have any?"

Tom knew he didn't have any lamb chops left; in fact, he was just about out of everything back in the meat case.

"No," he said. Then he lied, "I have had a big run on lamb chops today and I sold the last ones I had just ten minutes ago."

"Well, darn," she said. "How about a nice beef roast? Do you have any of those?"

Old Tom Fink realized that he must be looking pretty bad to her about now so he pretended to look under the meat counter in the cold box.

"No. I had ten or twelve really nice beef roasts earlier today, but I sold them all out by noon," he said, trying to impress her.

The prim old lady wrinkled her nose in disgust and said, "What kind of store is this? Don't you keep anything that a body could get to fix for Sunday dinner? I knew I should have just driven into Elizabeth to Barnes Store. They always have a good supply of meat."

Tom felt the red creeping up the back of his neck when he thought of the one frying hen that was left in the ice below the counter.

" Why sure I have some quality meat. In fact, I have got some grade A fresh frying hens just in this morning. That would make a great Sunday dinner. You could fry one up, make some gravy, mash some taters' and fix a mess of green beans. And I'll bet you are a terrific baker. Why don't you bake a peach or apple cobbler? That would make a fine meal for your preacher and his wife."

Tom studied her face to see if his sales pitch was working and to his delight, he saw her face light up.

"Why you know, my peach cobbler is well-known in our neck of the woods. And I do fry a mean chicken, if I do say so myself," she beamed. "Yes, I believe a good frying hen would do fine."

So Tom reached down in the ice and swished around like he was looking for that one special chicken. While doing this he said, "Well, let me see if I can find the best one in the box for you."

Then he grabbed the one, lonely hen out of the ice and slapped it up on the big meat scale.

"4 and ¾ pound," he said.

The lady thought deeply out loud, "4 and ¾ pound...4 and ¾ pound. I don't know if that is quite big enough. You got another one down in there?"

Tom Fink lied, "Oh, why yes! I have plenty of good, fresh chicken!"

He threw the chicken back into the ice and swished around again, then brought the same little hen out and slapped it up on the scale and slyly added his thumb onto the scale with it.

"6 pounds even!" Tom waited, confident that he had finally made the sale. The lady wondered out loud again.

"6 pounds even...6 pounds even," she thought.

Tom quickly chimed in, "6 pounds should be plenty of chicken for Sunday dinner."

She looked at Tom Fink and said, "Well, I want to make sure I have plenty so you'd better give me both of those hens.

Li'l Bits of Country Wisdom

Aunt Carolyn is truly an amazing woman of many talents and I am proud to be her husband. One of her greatest talents is that of introspection. She has the God-given ability to look at any situation that life may present and find the lesson within. For all of the talkin' that is done on the back porch, sometimes the simple words of wisdom carries the deepest message. I have included a few of Carolyn's words of wisdom for you to ponder as you go about your day.

Love and kindness comes from the heart,
not the wallet.

Every second of your life becomes your past, present, and future,
so why waste time when all you have is seconds to live.

You must be able to like, love, and respect yourself
before you can share these emotions with others.

Kind words can build a strong foundation;
harsh words can tear it down before it can be built.

Take away video games, you'll still win,
Take away cell phones, you can still talk,
Take away computers, you can still learn,
Take away family, you will lose.

If you see someone without a smile,
give them yours.

Learn to look at the positive, good things in life,
for when you do, you'll finally see just how
truly wealthy you really are.

Happiness is a disease and there are some who
will do everything in their power to cure you of it.

Take time to say "thank you," even to your spouse.

The person you truly are is when you're alone.

Be not what others think you should be,
but what your heart shows others you are.

Everyone is rich in their own way,
yet people let dollar signs cover their eyes.

Take time to smell the roses, but watch out for the thorns.

Wisdom is knowledge put to use after
all mistakes have been made.

Everything you do leads to the next step in your life;
however, sometimes you may have to walk backwards.

To believe in things that you cannot see nor understand
is the foundation for having faith.

Share good times and good news with others.
Leave the garbage in the gutter where it belongs.

A man can climb a mountain on his own, but how much
better it is to have someone to reach the top with.

Bring to the table good friends, family love, and a hearty laugh,
and you'll be filled to the brim.

It is not up to us to know what the next day will bring;
however, it is up to us to greet it with
perseverance, wisdom, gratitude, and happiness.

Not everyone will be a scholar or an artist, for what would the
world be like without constructions workers or farmers?

Even though others frown at you, exercise your right to smile.
It will catch on; just keep doing it!

Neither a lender nor borrower be without the help of each
other agreeing on what to lend or borrow.

A person may have a large family and many friends, however,
there is always one friend that is dearer to our hearts and sticks
closer than ever a brother or sister could.

Blessings are miracles in disguise.

To err is human, but to keep making the same mistakes
over and over is just plain stupid.

You may think you got by with that little white lie, but someday
the truth will come out. It always does.

Believe with all your heart you can and you will
accomplish anything you desire.

A poor man dreams of many riches;
A rich man forgets how to dream.

Everyone is kneaded out of the same dough,
but not baked in the same oven.

Saying thanks is easy, showing gratitude, well....
that's another story.

Remember to give thanks not just one day out of the year
but every day.

Never promise more than you can provide.

Tell me and I'll forget.
Show me and I may not remember.
Involve me and I'll understand.

The road less traveled is the one that will make
others wished they went there before you.

For every "bump in the road" there's a smooth
stretch of open highway that follows.

Life is truly what you make it. Each day brings new choices,
new experiences, and new projects.
So don't let your life pass you by for you'll never know
what you have missed.

Be mindful of the bridges you burn, for you may want to cross
them again someday.

When moving forward, take a few steps backward for you may
have missed something along the way.

Back Porch Talkin'

About the author:

William "Uncle Bill" Hornickel received his B.S. and M.S. in Secondary English Education and Journalism from Indiana University and completed a writing fellowship through the Indiana University Southeast Writing Project. During the completion of his writing fellowship, William discovered his affection for writing about his farm heritage and rural history through the voices of the many characters from his childhood.

This farm boy-turned-high school English teacher's love of rural heritage and history is evident in his recollections of 50 years of growing up and living on a farm in Southern Indiana. During his youth, Uncle Bill studied the art of storytelling and yarn-spinning from the many unique people that surrounded him, spending hour after hour listening to the older folks sharing gossip and tall-tales. William's unique commentary style and country-born introspection is a product of that rural up-bringing and the hours spent in the company of the many rural characters from his past, ultimately giving birth to Back Porch Talkin'.

Some of Uncle Bill's earliest farm memories are rooted in his love and passion for old tractors, an affection that he lovingly refers to as a "Tractor Thing." It was also during his rural adolescent years that Uncle Bill met his alter ego, Wally P. Hoglash; a naïve, simple-minded, good-old-boy from down-on-the-farm whose basic views on life offer a unique perspective and voice to what livin' country truly means.

Uncle Bill still resides on the family farm with his wife, Carolyn, who provides her insight on life through *Little Bits of Country Wisdom*. Each year, Aunt Carolyn and Uncle Bill make numerous appearances on the Back Porch Talkin' sound-stage, taking his unique style of country humor and commentary out to live audiences all around southern Indiana. In addition to his writing and teaching, he still works the family farm with his dad, Ralph, raising corn, soybeans, hay, horses, and cattle. As Uncle Bill is fond of saying: "Back Porch Talkin' isn't just a bunch of stories; it is a way of life!"

File# BPT 3-2-C4-F